GLASGOW UNDERGROUND

Keith Anderson

The history of the Subway is part of the history of Glasgow
and it deserves to be better known.
[Robert Gibson & Sons, 1905]

In dedication to the men with vision and ambition who persisted with their plan to
build a Subway in Glasgow and in respectful memory of those who paid dearly for
progress: John Ledingham and Alex Rogers who died in the course of tunnelling works
near Govan, September 1894.

First published 2014

Amberley Publishing
The Hill, Stroud
Gloucestershire, GL5 4EP

www.amberley-books.com

ISBN 978 1 4456 2174 6
EBOOK ISBN 978 1 4456 2189 0

British Library Cataloguing in Publication Data.
A catalogue record for this book is available from
the British Library.

Typeset in 9.5pt on 12pt Celeste.
Typesetting by Amberley Publishing.
Printed in the UK.

Contents

About this book

Hopefully this book will encourage you to visit and travel on the Glasgow Subway, or if you are a user it explains why the Subway continues to serve only the original Victorian era circle. Highly recommended is a visit to Glasgow Riverside Museum, where they have cleverly reconstructed a period tenement street scene complete with Subway station featuring Victorian era cars that you can go inside and explore. Traveling by Subway enables visitors to Glasgow to cram a lot in, seeing not only Subway locations but also places of interest such as: Scotland Street School Museum, Cessnock, with Alexander 'Greek' Thomson buildings, Cowcaddens is near the famous Charles Renne Mackintosh Glasgow School of Art building, Kelvinbridge offers city parking access and after all that why not take a break in Govan or a coffee at the old Company St Enoch HQ. Partick station is less than fifteen minutes' walk to the Riverside Museum.

If you plan to take photographs please remember the Subway is not a gimmick. It remains very much a working environment and passengers, drivers and other staff have a right to privacy. Please respect the SPT ban on the use of flash photography.

Above: St Enoch Square Subway Station from the railway station, *c.* 1905. *(Raphael Tuck & Sons)*
Left: Glass safety barriers at Ibrox Station. *(Author)*
Below: Natural light at Bridge Street, 1974. *(Hugh Hood)*

Introduction

Trains have been continually running beneath Glasgow since 1896; locals steadfastly refer to their wee railway as the 'Subway', its carriages are called 'cars'. When Glasgow District Subway Company launched the then cutting-edge urban rapid transport railway, it was one of Scotland's top infrastructure projects, second only to the Forth Rail Bridge in cost and only the third such underground railway in the world after the 1890 opening of Budapest's and the City & South London Railway. Proudly proclaiming itself to be the 'World's first cable hauled Subway', it was to remain such until electrification. Another unique aspect was its inability to breakout of the original tight circle and serve new parts of the city. This book charts and illustrates the Glasgow Subway from the city's frantic Empire growth days, its acquisition by the City through peak patronage to periods of make do and mend, near closure and salvation through public infrastructure investments. Specifically exploring the innovation, developments, key people, factors and events which shaped this railway and enable it to continue benefiting the areas it has passed under for some 120 years.

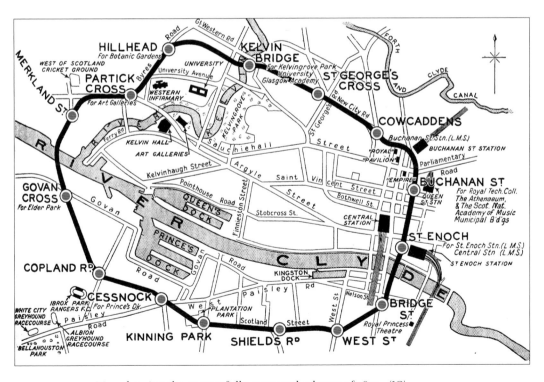

Map showing the successfully approved scheme of 1890. *(JC)*

1: Glasgow Second City of the Empire

Glasgow's meteoric rise to the status of 'Second City in the Empire' arose principally in Queen Victoria's reign, an era otherwise known as Britain's 'imperial century'. In terms of city development this was to be Glasgow's good times, characterised by unprecedented economic growth sustained through a series of unique factors and circumstances.

If population growth is an indicator of development then Glasgow's spectacular growth from 77,000 in 1801, swelling to 275,000 in 1841; by Victoria's death in 1901 numbers exceeded 760,000, thus ranking the city among the largest in the world and through trade also among the wealthiest. The population growth came from three principal sources: natural increased birth rate, city boundary extensions and more significantly massive immigration. In the early 1800s the Scottish Borders and Highlands were over-populated, under-employed and in comparison to central Scotland impoverished. Immigration was initially a localised drift from the rural hinterlands that significantly increased with greater railway penetration. The Irish famine of 1879 turned that trickle in to a flood, as previously temporary harvest labour stayed on or returned with their families as permanent migrants; about a third of Irish emigrants to Scotland settled in Glasgow.

Politically, as a result of Britain's Imperial expansion, Glasgow's growth secured an abundance of raw materials from colonies obliged to deal exclusively with British merchants operating British built and crewed vessels. Produce such as tobacco, sugar, rum and cotton was not only shipped in and out, all processing was local ensuring further retention of wealth. Indeed a significant part of Europe now relied upon Glasgow to replenish their growing tobacco demand.

Enviable geography also played it's part in the city's growth. Natural circumstances included: abundant coal and iron ore deposits within easy river and rail access. Fresh water has rarely been in short supply in Scotland but the Cites population had outgrown the local supply.

Since fresh water was seen as vital for industry and meeting the demands of a booming healthy population, the city's corporation demonstrated much foresight in taking water supply in to public ownership with the technically accomplished gravity fed connection from Loch Katrine and the city, about thirty miles distance. With this development, Glasgow enjoyed what was believed to be the finest water supply of any city anywhere in the world, indeed after opening in 1860 not only was a more reliable source of supply procured for thirsty industries but significantly typhoid and cholera were virtually eradicated.

The River Clyde, of course, was the vital geographical feature of Glasgow; the river was a superhighway, an artery through which the raw materials came and lucrative finished goods departed. Critical to everything was the river's navigability. Until 1857 Glasgow had to rely upon expensive trans-shipping from the lower Clyde ports. Between 1770 and 1857 a then unprecedented three million pounds was invested in dredging the Clyde making it possible for large ships to dock near the city. This investment soon paid off by enabling direct docking close to the city, thus saving transhipping. These cumulative advantages and impacts enabled Glasgow to grow rapidly, perhaps the most crucial at the time was the city's access to cheaper energy than its rivals.

> Transport and power are essentials of any economy. If a nation is to grow richer, progress in her agriculture and industry will soon exert pressure upon her sources of power and transport for similar improvements, and if they are not forthcoming progress will stop.
> [Charles Hadfield, *British Canals*, 1959]

Before the railways Scottish land transit was somewhat unreliable and expensive, disjointed and reserved only for the minority who could afford stagecoach fares. Limited localised ferries were reasonable alternatives as was passage (from 1788) along the Forth & Clyde Canal. The railway boom brought Glasgow the now familiar scramble of rival railway companies competing vigorously for land access and right of way to densely populated centres and key facilities such as mines and docks. By 1842 Glasgow had rail connections with Edinburgh, Greenock and Ayr. Before Central and St Enoch railwaysstations were opened, the rivalry centred on access issues concerning the shared Bridge Street station, just south of the Clyde. Within a few years local rivalry resulted in four close but separate rail terminals on the north side of the Clyde all offering speedy travel to destinations throughout Scotland and England. This masked a peculiar reality that Glasgow's terminal stations did not offer much transit capability within city boundaries, due to their lack of close to city feeder stations the absence of interchange between various railway Companies did not improve matters.

Local mainline railway operation did appear skewed towards serving medium to long distance, and it was 1886 before the south-side Cathcart circle suburban line opened. As the number of distant destinations grew and distance barriers were removed, so the numbers of inward migrants grew. Glasgow, like many Victorian cities, was somewhat socially polarised. On the one hand Glasgow Green, a great philanthropic gesture opened in 1900 as the first open public park space in the world; yet on the other hand limited low-cost housing for the impoverished immigrants led to squalid living conditions and landlord exploitation, earning the city's slums the unenviable reputation as the *'filthiest in Britain'*. For a time Glasgow was considered to be among the unhealthiest British cities, with the worst incidences of overcrowding, disease and poverty. As the city grew, so did its reliance upon coal for both heat and power creating belching pollution that soiled the air. In the slums respiratory conditions such as tuberculosis accounted for a third of all deaths in 1870.

For Glasgow's working classes, like elsewhere, constituted the majority of the city's population, and short distance rapid transit was not an option. Local public transport was in its infancy, limited to horse-drawn omnibuses or Clyde ferry locations served by the swift steam powered Clutha ferries, introduced in 1884. By 1870 local horse-drawn omnibus services featuring distinctive tartan liveries had begun to serve key points within the city and were proving popular, especially during rush hours, when overcrowding was an early sign that the various operators just could not cope with peak demand. Horse omnibuses were supposedly restricted to nineteen persons per horse. This was hardly mass transit and certainly fell short of rapid. Their relatively high cost precluded use by the lower paid working classes, who were forced to work near home or move closer to the breadwinner's workplace. Indeed this was still the era of the householder returning home for lunch, thus walking to work constituted the main means of transport at the time.

As industrialisation brought with it demands for specialist and semi-skilled workers to travel further afield, all this was about to change. New industries had begun to sprout up all over the city, generally increasing travel distances beyond reasonable walking distance. One historian remarked:

> Glasgow was an exceptional case, where suburban life ... owed less to rail connections than other cities. The middle class residential areas were too close to the centre for rail services to be attractive, and the rapidly growing working class 'suburbs' such as Maryhill, Partick or Bridgton likewise were very close to the centre and within reasonable walking distance for those with employment there.
>
> [John R. Kellett, *Railways and the Victorian Cities*]

Glasgow was originally confined to the north bank of the Clyde but demands to satisfy land-hungry housing, docks, industrial and commercial premises, ensured development would spill over to the south side, thus adding to distances and the infrastructure demand for river crossing points and cheap, efficient means of transport and communications. The first major step towards cheap transit for all, in the inter-urban sense, came from the tramways.

The Government, both at local and national levels, had by now learned from their mistakes with regards to the early canals and railways (1840s onwards) and early omnibus legislation – or the lack of it. Strict conditions had to be accepted by the prospective Companies wishing to obtain tramway or railway rights, including ensuring the finance was there to finish the project. Glasgow's first horse-drawn tramway opened in 1872, operated on an initial twenty-two year lease by the Glasgow Tramway & Omnibus Company (GTOC).

The horse tram moved large numbers of people relatively quickly and efficiently, they were a significant and recognisable step towards the mass transit we enjoy today. However, they were slow. Towards the end of the 1880s many European tram lines switched to electric working but many British tramway companies, such as in Glasgow, refused to electrify. The reason was, in part, because they only leased the local authority owned tram lines. British tram companies had to maintain their section of the road. In the GTOC case considerable resources had been expended in amalgamations and takeovers, leaving little for investment, and despite the benefits of increased speed and reduced cost such investment was still considered risky.

Glasgow was not unique; London traffic congestion in the 1860s was worse. Likewise London railway terminals were prevented from penetrating the heart of the City due to high density development. The solution in London was the novel underground Metropolitan Railway which, when completed, provided for rapid and inhibited transit between terminals. Glasgow's similarly high density streets were a similar barrier for Scottish railway companies, and added to the fact that two major railway companies had only just managed to squeeze into new central terminal, this meant that examining the potential offered by underground rail appeared to be the only feasible option.

Occupying the crown of the road, stopping repeatedly to pick up and set down passengers in the middle of the road. Not surprisingly trams were considered a 'great

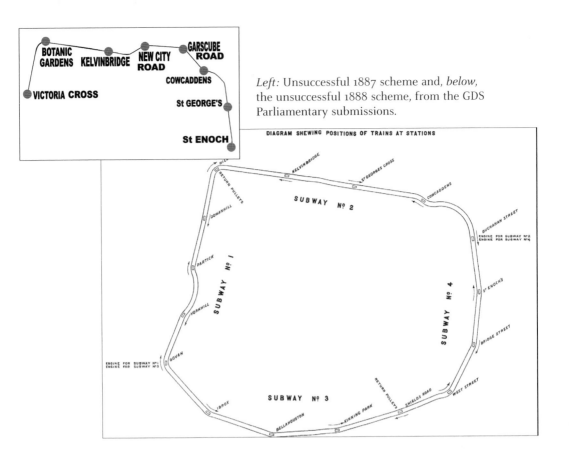

Left: Unsuccessful 1887 scheme and, *below,* the unsuccessful 1888 scheme, from the GDS Parliamentary submissions.

nuisance' by other vehicular traffic, especially on main thoroughfares and the few river crossings. The net result was that at peak times the city's bottlenecks were choked almost to standstill with competing mixed traffic. Yet despite their leisurely pace, Glasgow Tramways reported sales of 42 million tickets in 1888. Clearly transit capable of catering to the needs of the masses was big business.

Around 1887, amid the city's worsening congestion, a number of well to do citizens formed a likeminded group with the view of investigating the possibilities of constructing an efficient underground public transport system. In the main they were driven by investment and business opportunity rather than philanthropic aims.

By now underground travel was an acceptable mode for Londoners: the Thames Tunnel had opened in 1841, the cable-hauled (briefly) Tower Subway in 1870, and by 1886 the City & South London Railway Company had begun construction of their Stockwell to London tunnel (3½ miles) using the then innovative Greathead shield tunnelling method. Not only was going underground the only feasible solution in a highly developed metropolis, but it was an already accepted modus operandi for railway companies and therefore for the public. Indeed the Glasgow Central Railway (later part of the Caledonian Railway) followed the separate North Clyde line's example, securing powers in 1888 to traverse the city from Maryhill (north-west) to Rutherglen (south-east); both were east to west lines north of the Clyde. The era of underground travel had clearly reached Glasgow.

2: Glasgow District Subway Company 1887–1923

Parliamentary approval

By 1887 the interest group had taken advice from local civil engineering partners Simpson & Wilson C. E. concerning the suitability of subsoil and possible routes. They were encouraged enough to form themselves into a company which promptly submitted a Parliamentary Bill seeking approval to connect the centre of the city with the fashionable western residential area of Botanic Gardens on the Great Western Road, about three miles north-west of the city.

1887 scheme

The proposal was for a single tunnel 12 feet in diameter, featuring two interlaced 4 foot 8½ inch gauge tracks that would separate at stations situated at uniform 700 yard spacing. Cable traction was to be employed, but no drivers, since a solitary controller would periodically release a 700 yard displacement thereby moving all cars on precisely one station, with no perceived risk of collision and absolutely minimal staffing. Eight stations were envisaged, commencing at St Enoch Square proceeding to St George's, followed by stations at New City Road (Cowdaddens) Garscube Road, Kelvinbridge, Botanic Gardens terminating at Byre's Road, west of Victoria Street. The estimated cost of construction was £200,532. The House of Lords approved the Bill, but the Commons rejected it after hearing opinion from the Board of Trade together with objections from Glasgow Tram Company and the Caledonian Railway.

1888 scheme

The following year, 1888, the company presented a second and more ambitious Bill. This time the plan sought approval for a roughly circular route, as before built entirely underground, but with two separate twin-tunnels. The St Enoch to Partick routing together with the standard gauge remained. Both ends then extended south under the River Clyde to form the circle upon linking up on the fast developing south bank of the river. Although the route was well short of being as comprehensive as the then tram network that served Glasgow, it was well thought out and sought to capitilise upon several emerging commuter runs. Between the well to do western suburbs and the city, offering a rapid link between Govan and Partick, north side housing to south side docks and factories and emerging south side suburbs and the city.

As with London's Metropolitan line, the Glasgow planners identified the need to create links between the various rival railway terminals. St Enoch's square afforded access to the Glasgow & South Western Railway's similarly named terminal, and likewise both Buchanan and Queens Street rail terminals were easily reached from Buchanan Street proposed Subway Station. On the south side the original plan would have located Bridge Street Subway's access directly beneath the very active Bridge Street Railway terminals this included the Caledonian together with Glasgow & South Western Railways.

The proposed route clearly offered potential users the benefits from a quicker uninhibited underground journey rather longer walks to ferry points or split tram and ferry journeys. Costs were estimated at £677,000. But despite having the backing of the Lord Provost, together with support from all the route's Burghs, the Commons again rejected the Bill. The reason this time was not any concern regarding traction or the predictable self-interested competitor aspects, but rather objections of the Clyde Navigation Trustees. The Trustees were concerned about a perceived threat to the potential future river deepening posed by the Govan to Yorkhill section under the Clyde. The Clyde remained the recognised source of the City's continued prosperity and thus the trusties won the day.

1890 scheme

The proprietors were about to revive their original plan, effectively abandoning the single tunnel concept and Clyde crossings, when in 1889, the Glasgow Harbour Company, which had close association with the Clyde Navigation Trustees, obtained the powers to construct a short pedestrian and vehicular tunnel beneath the river at Finnieston. The significance of this was more in the legal precedence created by tunnelling under the Clyde. The Glasgow District Subway seized the opportunity to represent a similar Bill in 1890 this secured approval but did contain some costly clauses.

The Glasgow Subway Railway Company investor prospectus of 26 September 1890 stated: 'the Company was incorporated to construct a circular railway 6½ miles in length through the North Western, Central and South Western Districts of Glasgow'. It appears cable traction was very much in favour even at this stage, the prospectus referring to traction as 'by such means other than steam locomotives'.

Appointing engineering expertise

The subsequent Parliamentary Act of 1891 envisaged the use of standard gauge (4 feet 8½ inches) in the twin-tunnel line. The line was to connect sixteen stations: St Enoch Square, West George Street, Buchanan Street, Cowcaddens, St George's Cross, River Kelvin, Ashton Terrace (Hillhead) Downhill Street, Merkland Street, Govan Cross, Brighton Street (Copland Road), Walmer Crescent (Cessnock), Cornwall Street, Shields Road, West Street and Eglinton Street.

Key technical knowledge was assured with the formal appointment of Alexander Simpson's firm Simpson & Wilson as consulting civil engineers. Simpson brought his expansive mining and overseas railway experience, but more significantly he had worked on the City & District Railway (1886) and with the Finneston Tunnel; he therefore knew better than anybody the strata that were likely to be encountered under Glasgow. It is not without significance that he was also amongst the principal shareholders of the enterprise and would later become chairman of the company, his partner Walter Wilson would also take a directorship. The Subway was also in need of a consulting mechanical and electrical engineer this took the form of the appointment of David Hume Morton C.E.

Choice of traction

Morton had travelled widely in order to thoroughly investigate all traction options. Steam locomotion had been eliminated as a choice pre-Bill stage. The public's dislike of such obnoxious conditions was proven with the Metropolitan line in London. This led to a Board of Trade inquiry into levels of carbon dioxide and sulphur in its tunnels. The example of the Caledonian's new Central low-level line was to confirm the local displeasure for steam traction in tunnels and the line was never popular. This left the choice between electric or cable traction. At the time electric motors, which a significant number of the company's backers were keen on pursuing, were considered too large for the space offered by the diminutive sized bogie and in any case it appears that the motors available lacked sufficient power to handle the demands, such as the climbs of 1:40 approaching stations and also the under Clyde climb of 1:20. Morton describes the choice of cable traction:

> A few words may be devoted to the reasons of adopting a cable traction system for the Subway. The chief promoters, and the chief engineers of the road, Simpson & Wilson C.E. had selected the cable system and did not weaver in their opinion that the line should be put in to operation as a cable railway. ['Glasgow District Subway, its construction plant and working', Andrew Hume Morton 1897]

But perhaps the factor that influenced the proprietors above all else to opt for cable were the perceived efficiency gains, created in part by the choice of a circular route and its various inclines under the river crossings. Here cable held a significant technical and operational advantage. Trains travelling down inclines exerted a positive balance by gravity against the trains travelling up inclines in the opposite direction. This natural cancelling out of haulage power would thus be an efficiency factor that actually increases as more trains are introduced to the circuit. Tram or surface steam by contrast, meant that with the introduction of each additional car or set the operational costs increased proportionally. This gravitationally derived benefit meant that stations either side of river crossings could be built nearer to the surface, itself a construction saving and a passenger benefit.

> The use of cable haulage was no freak to be dispensed with as soon as any funds were available. It was a thoroughly sound proposition and although the speed of transit was slow compared with later standards of underground travel it served the City of Glasgow for no less than thirty-eight years.
> [O. S. Nock, *Underground Railways of the World*]

Indeed besides cable worked coal mines, Scotland also had some early success with cable traction assisting departing locomotives out of Queen Street Station's steep climb and also with the cable-hauled trams in Edinburgh.

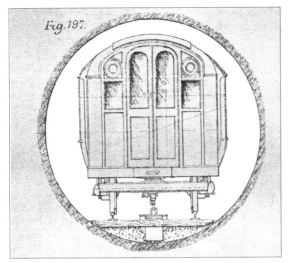 

Above left: End view of cablecar in 11-foot diameter tunnel, with 9-inch ceiling clearance. *(Engineering, March 1897) Above right:* Miners working in a similar sized London tunnel. *(The Engineer, 1895)*

Choice of track gauge

Track gauge refers to the distance or width between the rails. A Royal Commission's findings on competing gauges resulted in the Gauge Act of 1846 which stipulated that new passenger-carrying railways in Britain should be built to a 'standard' gauge of 4 feet 8½ (or 143.5 cm), however, this ruling did not apply to so-called 'narrow gauge' or light railways, a fact not lost on the Subway Company. Choice of track gauge was a critical factor for any railway venture of the time, since it was key to the track engineering and the ease, or otherwise, of linking up with adjoining railways. The Subway Act of 1890 stipulated the adoption of 'standard gauge of 4 feet 8½ inches, but critically this was later amended to 'not less than 3 feet 6 inches' in the subsequent 1894 Act.

With no locomotives to support, the company could also use lighter gauge rail, thus the 60 lb per yard rail was a sensible choice given the assumed loads. The company decided upon the adoption of an unusual gauge of 4 feet (122 cm), one not shared by any surface railway near Glasgow. The rational for this decision has been the subject of much debate ever since; however it was effectively the widest gauge that could be accommodated by an 11-foot wide tunnel. London's smaller underground tunnels standardised on an 11-foot 8-inch minimal bore enabling them to accommodate a wider gauge. The Glasgow company's choice of gauge must therefore be aligned with their choice of an 11-foot tunnel width. The cut-and-cover approach to tunnelling offered variation in tunnel width, but not so with shield tunnelling, it was precise and had to work with predetermined cast iron sections made to match the shield's diameter. It may be that the answer lay in the choice of a smaller shield which, theoretically at least, offered a greater tunnelling speed and therefore shorter construction time. The full implications of adopting such an unusual gauge would have a significant impact upon the prospects of the venture, but this was not to become clear until some thirty years later.

Tunnel construction

The two most popular means of tunnel construction in Victorian times were cut-and-cover and the shield method. Cut-and-cover was the popular railway method, whereby one dug up all the ground in the projected line of the track and after making a secure base for the rail sleepers, then applied the wall and ceiling. Simpson's design was 'horse shoe' in shape utilising concentric brickwork, four rings on the arch and two on the walls, before filling in and levelling the ground at surface level. Where rock was encountered a passageway was blasted through and a concrete lining, 18 inches thick, was applied. The shield method was originally a Marc Isambard Brunel invention in 1818. It was subsequently enhanced first by Peter W. Barlow and again by James Henry Greathead, then the Civil Engineer for the City & South London Railway in 1884.

The shield was slower but did not require the necessity of digging up an entire street and displacing surface traffic. Progress through strata used the principal of thrust against the existing tunnel wall segments, usually 1 inch thick cast iron sections, and navigating along the chosen route by manipulating the various thrust settings. In this case, thrust was provided by six hydraulic rams in each shield unit capable of exerting a thrust of up to 2,200 lbs, although rarely more than 800 lbs was required throughout its use under Glasgow due to the generally lose strata encountered near rivers.

The Company had allowed for five years to conclude all the works, cut-and-cover would be preferable following where possible the street pattern. At the time geology under Glasgow was not widely appreciated; the proximity of the river ensured that alluvial strata would be encountered. *The Engineer* subsequently reported the conditions thus:

The material encountered was, as a whole, bad, as the following schedule by Mr Robert Simpson, BSc, CE, shows:

Govan to Partick West, 2,800 feet, under river Govan side sand; Partick side, mud; under river, rock and boulder clay.

Partick West to Partick East, 2,155 feet, clay hard rock, shale, and old coal waste.

Partick East to Hillhead, 1,994 feet, shale and sandstone.

Hillhead to Kelvin Bridge 2,948 feet shale and sandstone.

Kelvin Bridge to St George's Cross, 2,588 feet, shale and sandstone.

St George's Cross to Cowcaddens, 2,314 feet, shale and sandstone with soft clay opposite the Normal School.

Cowcaddens to Buchanan Street, 2,610 feet, sandstone and shale.

Govan to Copland-road, 3,007 feet, sand and muddy sand and clay.

Copland-road to Cessnock, 2,182 ft., muddy sand and clay.

Cessnock to Kinning Park 1,614 feet, muddy sand.

Kinning Park to Shields Road, 2,671 feet, sand and muddy sand.

Shields-road to West Street, 1,964 feet brick clay.

West-street to Bridge-street, 1,710 feet brick clay.

Bridge-street to St Enoch, 2, 204 feet sand.

St Enoch to Buchanan Street, 1,819 feet, sand with sandstone near St George's Church.

[Extract from the *Engineer* 4 December 1896]

Above: Tunnel interior with typical cable support shelf. *(MacLure, MacDonald & Co.)*

Construction commenced in March 1891, by the digging of a major pit at St Enoch's Square from which tunnelling both northwards and southwards could simultaneously begin, in both tunnels. Water was encountered only 15 feet down. The plan was to deploy shield construction wherever water was encountered, since if maintained the tunnel head even in porous conditions using bolted iron castings was more efficient than having construction labour idle while bricks and mortar set.

The cast iron segments were 'U' shaped in profile, and it took ten such segments to make up the tunnel circle of 11 feet at any given point. Tar was used as a water sealant, both between the segments and the strata outside of the tunnel, with the segments bolted together at the flanges. Three thicknesses were used: ¾ inch (19 mm) general use. Slightly heavier gauge 1 inch (25 mm), used under the Clyde crossings, also under the Glasgow Central Railway crossing. Finally, the thickest gauge of 1.125 inch (28 mm) was reserved for use beneath the Caledonian and Glasgow & South Western railways at Pollokshields. A total of 120,000 segments, weighting about 20,000 tons, were employed in the undertaking. The iron was required to stand a tensile strain of 6½ tons per square inch and of 2½ tons per square inch without loss of elasticity whilst bars 1 inch square stood a load of 7 cwt., applied at the centre of a 3-foot span without fracture. About 29% of construction used the shield technique, due to the combination of saturated water strata and the tram operator's success in persuading the City, to place clauses in the Act that limited the length and duration of street disturbance.

Due to the wet riverside conditions, tunnel access entrances had to be sealed so as to enable high pressure working. This helped to stem the flow of mud and water onto the workforce. At the entrance to such workings an air lock had to be used, often in the order of 20 feet long, to allow the entry of wagons to retrieve the ground being eaten out by the tunnel's advance. Under river construction was the riskiest part of this enterprise, since the Thames Tunnel had suffered a catastrophic collapse leading to the original proprietor's bankruptcy. If anything, conditions under the Clyde were worse than that experienced under the Thames.

Sixteen shields (supplied by Markham of Chesterfield) were deployed in tunnel construction. In all, five classifications of construction technique were deployed by Simpson summarised:

1. Ordinary cut-and-cover
2. Underpinning under air pressure, the material being capable of being drained only with considerable difficulty, or not at all
3. Iron tunnelling without air, in cases where material impervious to water was found, where the surface was occupied, and where immunity from all subsidence was specially sought
4. Ordinary brick tunnelling, where material impervious to water was found with an occupied surface, but the possibility of repairing the damage at moderate cost should subsidence occur
5. Iron tunnelling under air pressure through water-logged strata at considerable depths.

In total 3,345 yards of tunnels were constructed by the shield method, the remaining 8,178 yards constructed in brick and concrete. A clause in the 1891 Act permitted the use of cut-and-cover only where the street was accessible to traffic and when under private property forbade the payment of 'wayright' fees. Thus making economic sense to follow the street pattern and reduce the company's exposure to costly and time consuming land purchase.

Tunnelling incidents

With the construction of the Subway the sub-surface railways caused much havoc with the tramways. The cut-and-cover methods forced omnibuses to change their routes. However, this was a little more difficult for the trams. Shield tunnelling was thus the tram company's preference, however, an incident above such Subway workings on the New City Road in July 1892 demonstrated how close Subway tunnels were to the surface. A horse tram was travelling along this section when suddenly the surface gave way with the horses disappearing into the gap below. Momentum ensured the tram continued to traverse over the hole on its thankfully intact rails. This bizarre incident concluded with the horses later being returned to the owners, from the nearest surface access. Obviously shield construction was active below and it is thought that the shield face had had been drawn back along the tunnel for servicing, therefore leaving the tunnel head temporally unsupported and vulnerable.

In alluvial strata it was necessary to deploy airlocks at site entrances and increase the air pressure so as to counter the in rush of water; this made demanding conditions even more blighted for the workers. Sometimes the resultant pressure was extremely uncomfortable for the tunnel head teams. Such high pressure was actually the cause of a 'blow out' incident under the Clyde in February 1894. Such flooding endangered the labourers in addition posing a serious set-back to the construction schedule.

Air pressure was a major problem if it got too high and if the ground above the tunnel could not contain it then 'blow outs' occurred. This was the cause near Custom

House Quay, where the bed of the river is only 14 feet deep from the top of the tunnel, and such blow outs occurred in succession for one blighted contractor. Finally a huge blow out occurred in February 1894, when a depression 24 feet square and 16 feet deep was blown in the bed of the river and the tunnels were immediately inundated. Sailors on nearby Custom House Quay were showered by small stones, causing them to flee up Dixon Street from their invisible foe. Fortunately no one was hurt but the contractor had endured enough and threw in his hand.

The successor contractor, George Talbot, patched the hole with an ingenious ½-inch curved steel plate and clay. Henceforth air pressure was regulated more carefully according to the depth of the soil cover and state of tide in the river. In 1895 a deputation was received from Paris Metro-line officials, keen to learn from Glasgow's river tunnelling experience, their fact finding ensured that the Paris Metro would bridge rather than tunnel beneath the Seine.

Fire posed a more serious danger and again contractor George Talbot was extremely lucky when one of his teams was trapped for some twenty-two hours in a tunnel fire near St Enoch's. At a time when there were no specialist rescue services, he led a successful rescue attempt from the adjoining tunnel to free his men. His rescue team dug and battered their way through to liberate their comrades. Sadly another fire, near Govan, in 1894 cost the lives of two of his men, who suffocated after a fire broke out in a pressurised tunnel section containing flammable materials. The cause of the fire was traced to naked candle use; thereafter only contained oil lamps were deployed in tunnels.

Sadly, such casualties were not uncommon in major engineering infrastructural projects of the day and no fewer than ninety-five souls were to be lost in the construction of the Forth Railway Bridge, for example, to say nothing of the apalling death toll among Britain's mining communities at the time. No records appear to have been compiled concerning prolonged exposure of the tunnel teams to pressurised conditions. No accounts speak of depressurising procedure, in fact to the contrary, one account talks of the men vacating the pressure workings for tea on the surface. There may well have been adequate procedure for the time, however, the decrompression chamber – the only effective procedure to avoid the 'bends' – was not invented until 1916. As recently as the early 1960s when the Clyde Road tunnel was built in similar depths near Govan two men were known to have died of the 'bends', it is thus feasible that in the late 1800s insufficient knowledge of this life-threatening condition was widespread.

Station construction

Station construction like tunnelling depended upon site conditions, and it was simply not feasible to open a great pit like that at St Enoch for all stations. Dug out station construction deployed much greater thickness of materials. Up to eight layers of bricks were used to arch over stations, or up to 30 inches of concrete on platform arches. Much of the rest of the station was built largely of wood. This includes the platforms and staircases; in some instances even the roofs were wooden. Of all the stations at street level, with the exception of St Enoch's station (a bespoke architect design) and West Street, all entrances were incorporated into the pre-existing tenement frontages.

Maintenance depot

The car works were located over the tunnels at Broomloan Road, near Govan Cross station. Because of the choice of cable traction it was impossible to include junctions, points or crossovers. Subway cars would be added and removed from the tracks via a crane located over the two tunnels. The crane was a 12 ton transversing model able to reach all rail lanes of the depot, and also acted as a turntable for the depot since there were no rail points. The carriages would routinely be hauled up to the depot for overhauls, with painting and spot checks carried out at night, and the running cars remaining parked in both tunnels between Copeland Road and Govan Cross stations.

When first constructed, the building was about 220 feet long and had an average width of 115 feet covering about 25,300 square feet. The whole area was open, with brickwork confined only to walls and offices at the works surface entrance. Roofs were supported by rivet style steel pillars and light steel lattice beams. The roof was glazed in a similar way to factory designs of the time.

Top: Recent view of Scotland Street Power Station frontage. *(Author)*
Left: Cable tension run building and carriages. *(MMD)*

Above: Main shaft rope drums, friction clutches and barring engine at Scotland Street Power House. *(MMD)*

Power station

Most of the Victorian era predated the electric grid, thus factories, hotels, and indeed all manner of business concerns, had to generate their own power. The Subway sited their powerhouse at a 1½ acre site in Scotland Street because the tunnels passed along that street and were mutually convenient to the tunnels and adjoining the Glasgow–Paisley joint railway line. This enabled cost-effective bulk delivery of coal supplies to the rear yard.

The apparatus was designed by Morton, the building by John Gordon I.A. This undertaking was a major feat of engineering in itself and somewhat cutting edge for its day. The complex consisted of a boiler house and main engine house, the tension runs and a store. The boiler house was the smaller of the two being 132 feet long and 88 feet wide and 23 feet high to the springing of the roof. The main engine house was 138 feet long and 100 feet wide and incorporated a 180-foot high chimney at its north corner. Down the centre of this building were located four heavy cast iron beams of 'H' section carrying the central travelling crane girders. Running northwards from the engine house to Scotland Street was the tension run and this was 193 feet long 33 feet wide and 18 feet 6 inches high. Adjoining this on the west was the stores building. The Station was in use from 1896 until 1935, when cable traction was replaced by electricity.

Top left: Side view of Scotland Street Powerhouse and tension run building.
Left: Boiler House, water tank and coal store, with Glasgow-Paisley Joint Railway visible to the *left.*
Below: One of the two main engines. *(MMD)*

Above: St Enoch Station and the company's head office in 1896. *(MMD)*

Route and station changes

The company's original goal of connecting the City to Botanic Gardens was impeded by the Glasgow Central Railway (GCR, later Caledonian Railway) being granted rights to build their line under that part of Great Western Road. Given that the 1890 Act required the Company to pay for 50 yards of construction either side of the same line under Argyle Street, and again under the joint line near Pollockshields, the costs of securing a Botanic Gardens Station would have been extremely prohibitive, especially since two passes of that line would be required in order to return under the Clyde. Instead Byres Road or Ashton Lane opened as Hillhead Station nearer the Great Western Road end of the Byres Road. Due to its proximity this led to Dowanhill Station being scrapped before construction commenced. Alterations were made to a number of station locations: Bellahouston became Cessnock, Yorkhill became Merkland Street, Partick became Partick Cross. Thus fifteen stations were built, all were located on the 6½ mile circuit and the average distance between stations was well under half a mile. This ensured that the majority of the zone inside the circle and to a distance of about one-third mile radius walk outside of it were within its 'catchment area'. The company estimated this catchment as 330,000 people at the time of construction. At no time did the Subway Company appear to consider expansion plans to include the highly populated eastern or northern suburbs, or even other populated concentrations similarly by passed by the railway; thus the proposed circle was to retain a definite western and near south bank bias.

Left: The 'Gripper' device and sample length of cable. *(Author)*
Below: Copland Road Station with cable visible between the rails. *Bottom:* Gripper Car No. 12 in the depot, *c.* 1896. *(MMD)*

3: First Subway Cars

Designed by David Morton, the first Subway cars featured a distinctive horseshoe end on profile. Internally, four bulkheads provided significant strengthening while also acting as aesthetic breaks on what otherwise appeared as a monotonous pair of full-length facing benches. GDS gripper cars were 40 feet 9 inches long. The framework of the body was of teak panelled in plywood, and the roof was timber clad with sheet zinc plate used to deflect tunnel seepage. This was built on a plate iron under-frame supporting two four-wheel bogies similar to the American car design of the era.

The end bulkheads allowed for the provision of a double sliding door arrangement, thus separating the passenger area from the noisy vestibules. Each vestibule featured a central manual sliding door at either end, to facilitate between-car access. The entrance doorway was guarded in motion by a collapsible trellis gate, fitted to one side only and regardless of which circle the train took the car's gates always faced the platform. Aesthetically there is also a vague resemblance to the similarly horseshoe shaped and diminutive City & South London carriages with the exception that Morton included larger window openings.

The cars featured novel electric lighting, the power being picked up by a small trolley style contact arrangement mounted on the opposite side to the entry doorway. This feature enabled the Company to claim they were the first railway to be fully equipped with such. The Board of Trade required the fitting of hand-brakes together with Westinghouse automatic air-brakes. Hand-wheels in the vestibules operated the hand-brakes while up front in the driver's vestibule the air-brake was intended for emergency use. Since cars did not carry their own compressors they were frequently topped up from an air supply held at West Street Station.

Oldbury Carriage & Wagon Co.

The first cars, thirty grippers, were built by the Oldbury Carriage & Wagon Company. They had negligible suspension, but fortunately journey times were short. The cars seated forty-two passengers on a similar configuration to the trams. The facing wooden bench arrangement was a renowned third-class seating feature and may have proven intolerable for prolonged distance surface travel.

The gripper device

Cable grippers were the 'clutch' mechanism by which the carriages were propelled. It was a critical mechanism and took drivers, or 'gripmen', some getting used to. The grip mechanism was mounted on the leading bogie under the leading axle. The grip was controlled by a horizontal hand wheel and lever. Ideally the wheel was used to apply or release speed without jerking. The lever, known as the 'trip' lever, was normally used once per circuit at the cross-over and it released pressure immediately while also pushing the cable clear of the grip unit. The grip unit itself was made of two iron castings, an upper and lower part, both sculpted to accept the 1½ inch cable. The lower one was set at a fixed height above rail level therefore making the adoption of the normal suspension units impossible. The upper unit was variable in height by the

23

hand wheel, thus applying pressure to the cable and gripping or releasing pressure and allowing it to pass freely through the grip. The lower die was tapered at the ends to facilitate the cables dropping off when required and also had a bar each end, 2 inches broad, which jumped up to allow the cable to be thrown off at the Scotland Street crossover.

The opening between the dies for inserting the cable was at one side only – the side furthest from the centre of the circle. Thus the cable would have no tendency to leave the grip on curves to the right on the Outer Circle and to the left on the Inner Circle, these being the common direction of curves on the circles. But there were reverse curves at Cowcaddens, Partick Cross and Cessnock in the opposite directions where the cable would tend to run towards the open side of the grip unit, and the driver had to release pressure carefully lest the cable were to leave the grip entirely.

Trailer cars

With the increasing traffic it soon became clear that single-car trains, even with occasional twin-car trains, could not cope with demand. The company ordered trailer cars in 1897 with all twenty-four delivered the following year from Hurst Nelson of Motherwell, again following Morton's specifications. These cars were only 25 feet long, in contrast to the previous 40-foot 9-inch long gripper units. The shorter saloon featured a single bulkhead with seated capacity being twenty-four rather than forty-two passengers. These cars were sufficiently light and short to enable one gripper car to haul two of them, an operational feature when heavy traffic was anticipated.

In anticipation of increasing traffic due to the Imperial Exhibition held in Kelvingrove Park in 1901, four additional bogie gripper cars were ordered. In 1902 the trailer cars, which had never been popular with the public due to their bumpy ride, were subsequently converted into twin-bogie full length trailer cars. A total of fourteen were converted, each having the same overall length as the gripper cars, and their shorter vestibules offered a longer saloon, providing an additional two seats. The remaining trailers were scraped prior to the arrival of the last two gripper cars in 1913/14. Amazingly, the majority of this fleet would continue to serve right up until the 1977 modernisation, ranking these carriages among the longest serving and best maintained carriages of the late Victorian era.

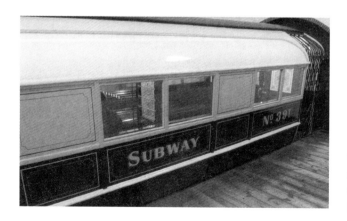

Trailer Car No. 39T at Riverside Museum with wooden platform. (Author)

4: Glasgow District Subway Co. 1896–1923

Cost overruns

Prolonged and ambitious engineering projects are prone to cost escalation, as was the case with the subway. In an effort to avert a looming cash crisis, the Glasgow District Subway (Further Powers) Act 1894 granted the company powers to raise a further £550,000 capital. This enabled compulsory purchase of the power station and car sheds, also extending the completion date by up to two years. Upon the completion of the powerhouse and with the delivery of the first subway cars, David Hume Morton was sufficiently satisfied with progress to approve running trials commencing in November 1896. Thus after a mammoth six years of non-stop costs, finally the prospect of revenue earning railway operations was beginning to dawn.

Preparations for opening

During the weeks prior to opening, the new cable cars that had arrived were trialled extensively, so as to accustom drivers, conductors and station staff to their operational roles. The cars were to operate on the principal of clockwise travel on the outer circle and anticlockwise on the inner. In the weeks preceding opening the company installed cutting edge lighting technology, enabling all cars to be electrically lit. The Board of Trade, who evaluated the safety aspects, were equally impressed with the carriage lighting, paying tribute to the brightness of the cars and the clean airy stations. Passenger safety was an utmost consideration and the Subway designers felt they had left absolutely nothing to chance, ensuring any train could be pulled up in

Below: Alexander Simpson plaque from St Enoch's concourse. *(Author)*

the distance of its own length, signals were worked automatically with all stations having telephone and bell tone connections with the next, as well as the powerhouse, in case of a need to stop one of the cables.

Semaphore signals worked by trip mechanisms at the entrance to each station meant that there was no need for signalmen. The Semaphore indicated the line ahead of the station was free. In the event of one train approaching the rear of another in a tunnel, each car had oil lamps mounted beside the centre doors to indicate its position, although the chances of cars colliding was considered remote, since the track speed is similar throughout, and no train could leave a station without a clearance signal.

The Subway opening

The company announced their opening for 5 a.m. on 14 December 1896. No pomp or ceremony associated, such a prestigious development was evident with modest adverts appearing in the morning editions merely advising the locations of stations. A possible explanation may be the Subway's prominence amongst the news columns of the day.

By that time only fourteen of the batch of thirty cable grip cars had been commissioned, seven allocated to each circle; they offered a four minute frequency rather than six, as had been the original intention. The 1d flat (adult) fare for any distance was payable at the turnstiles located at the foot of the station stairs. During trials the cars were run in pairs with the rearmost being a smoker.

Large queues of workers, eager to save time and a few pence, formed before the stations opened, they were joined by office and shop workers, all keen to be among

Below: Alexander Simpson, Walter Wilson and David Hume Morton, 1896. *(MMD)*

the first to ride on the new District Subway. Before daybreak, all stations were under siege with busy platforms and lengthening queues.

No one had anticipated the threat posed by 'joy-riders'. This took the form of passengers remaining on board the car way past their destination. Even those who were requested to vacate the car by a conductor tended to alight and immediately pass back through the turnstiles, thus avoiding lengthening queues for another go. Estimates suggested that 1,400 passengers had crammed into the then fourteen forty-six-seater cars in the first few hours alone.

Despite the higher demand the system actually coped well, until around mid-afternoon when a car approaching Buchanan Street failed to grip the cable properly, causing a 'cable jump', whereby the cable slips off a series of their support shelves. The Outer-circle cable had to be stopped immediately, resulting in passengers caught between stations having to fumble their way along the dark tunnels to the nearest station. This left the company reliant upon seven cars on the Inner Circle running at reduced speed attempting to cope with the high demand.

On the narrow platforms that were dangerously overloaded by waiting passengers to the extent that station staff were struggling to cope with demand, most were content to await their turn. Despite the best efforts of station staff to try and maintain order, some fraught rushes occurred. A particularly heavy mêlée at Bridge Street platform knocked over and injured a conductor.

With a few hours to go the system continued to perform, as an overcrowded car awaiting the signal to proceed to St Enoch was hit by the follow on car from Bridge Street, resulting in some twenty injured passengers, two seriously. The collision brought the line to a halt for the day, obliging passengers marooned in cars between stations to vacate along dark tunnels while attempting to avoid the continually running cable. The company were fortunate no fatalities occurred and the immediate closure was extended five weeks so that more robust alterations to working practices could be implemented.

Mr Morton had advised the company to wait for additional cars and, if they did proceed, to place all their fourteen cars onto the one Circle. However, his advice was ignored, resulting in risk not only to passengers but also the Subway's reputation. Perhaps it was the cumulative impacts of the poorer ground conditions, tunnel fires, the series of under Clyde 'blow-outs', and costly route avoidance near Botanic Gardens combined with the need to compulsory purchase additional property when burdened with the costs of recruiting operational staff that persuaded the owners to ignore sound advice.

The Subway did not reopen until 21 January 1897, by which time the Board of Trade were satisfied that new precautions would avert any repeat of the collision and derailment circumstances. Platform overcrowding was eliminated by substituting unmanned turnstiles with manned ticketing, the station manager could suspend sales and thus regulate the passenger numbers waiting at platform level. Joy riding was eliminated by staging the fare structure: 1d, for up to four stations, 2d thereafter. Despite this increase, the Subway still remained good value and the rapid Clyde crossings ensured the patronage of passengers located close to those stations. With the full complement of rolling stock delivered, the frequency was brought down to less than three minutes.

Operations

By the end of the first year's operations the Subway had transported 9,628,392 passengers. Patronage appeared to be on the up, implying a promising future. Indeed, at the time, the route of the Subway was well situated; it was very popular with those who wished to cross the Clyde since it avoided the now over busy Finniston Tunnel or city bridge bottlenecks, such as Jamaica Street Bridge then West along Scotland Street towards Govan and the busy Southside docks and shipbuilding yards. The evidence suggests a reasonable good balance of cross-town traffic was emerging, e.g. Partick to St Enoch took only fourteen minutes, as opposed to the fastest horse drawn tram route of over half an hour. In the first year's operation, with the large construction overheads yet to be paid off, the directors approved a modest dividend of ½ per cent to 1 per cent. The initial build estimate of £677,000 proved a gross underestimate; costs had soared to £1,680,000 about 2½ times the 1890 estimate. The premature opening did not help the finances; the Subway was obliged to absorb costs associated with satisfying the Board of Trade safety requirements, namely manned ticketing at all stations, an outlay turnstiles were meant to avoid, plus yet another month of no revenue.

Rise and fall in patronage

The first five years were very encouraging with patronage on the up; that trend continued until the end of 1918, thereafter enduring a sharp fall off. In fact, patronage would probably have fallen much earlier had the First World War not placed additional demands on local factories and yards within the subway's reach.

In Victorian Glasgow, employees were obliged to accept much longer working hours, in many cases without any weekend respite; therefore travel time was becoming an issue. The horse-drawn omnibus and trams just made distances of up to about two to three miles possible in fair traffic conditions but it was the Subway that first made commuting between the corners of the City it served more practicable. This had the effect of relieving many Glaswegians of the need to move nearer the location of their work.

In 1899 the company went to the shareholders to raise funds to pay for twenty-four new trailer cars in order to complement and increase the capacity of the existing trains. The Subway may have become quite a growing concern had it not been for the complete electrification of Glasgow's tramways by their new owner Glasgow Corporation. The Corporation's low fares municipal benefit ethos had the impact of artificially suppressing Subway fares. The tram electrification programme was completed in 1901, increasing tram speed to a credible 12 miles per hour, meaning that for the first time Subway patrons would have choices. Local demand for rapid transit although significant, had not grown to the point where it could viably support both trams and Subway. Even the surface railways were by now embarking upon their own station rationalisation and closures around the city, and after 1905, the Clutha boats departed the Clyde too.

Above: West Street station in 1896. *(MMD)*

Deteriorating finances

In his 1898 article Benjamin Taylor noted that the 'subway was not paying'. From the 1918 peak patronage of 20,970,000 passengers, only 7,922,000 were carried in 1922, yet the Company's overheads and expenses rose dramatically. The lost traffic can partly be placed at lower peacetime demand and the public's preference for the better point-to-point service offered by the expanding electric tram network. Under electric traction the Corporation-operated tram competition had the impact of precluding any subway fare increases for fear of further lost patronage; thus the reduced income could not cover their increased costs. In fact, in December 1916 the company was obliged to reintroduce the system-wide penny fare.

The running costs of the Subway were at first considerably less than for any given 6½ mile length of any London Underground railway. However, as a Board of Trade regulated railway the company was expected to fully resource its establishment which trams operators were unburdened with. By 1902 all of Glasgow's trams were electric running; their routes penetrated all new housing developments, and when not locked in city bottle necks they enjoyed higher average running speeds, yet always lower manning and overheads than the Subway. In contrast cable traction system relied upon a coal hungry powerhouse, was limited to 12½ miles per hour, and the entire system required specialist maintenance staff. Since the time consuming overhead crane process for the depot was only employed at night, in between rush hour periods, the fleet ran well under capacity since and unlike surface railways excess subway capacity could not be withdrawn without bringing their circle to a prolonged stoppage.

Dividends were incremental and the last was paid to ordinary shareholders in 1912. Preference shareholders received approximately 2 per cent return until 1918 simply because the company was not capable of sustaining anything further. Prior to the 1920s banks, having witnessed London's Underground wilting under their construction costs, had ceased supporting the Subway, thus to keep going directors offered personnel guarantees. Subsequently, employee wages fell behind inflation and labour relations worsened. Matters came to ahead in January 1920 with a five week strike over pay and hours. In the circumstances the subway's offer of a 6.19 per cent increase was possibly unaffordable given the competitive threat posed by the Corporation's electric trams. The dispute was only resolved after the threat of mass dismissal and the recruitment of new labour; such poor industrial relations would not have enhanced the company's reputation among the communities who would have already switched to trams in order to travel to their work.

Glasgow Subway, like most narrow gauge, cable-hauled or light-railways, was not included in the Railways Act of 1921. The formerly acquisitive mainline railways were only just recovering from the wartime coal shortages under Government control; they lacked the funds and in any case don't appear to have shown any overt interest in taking on the Glasgow Subway, despite the fact it clearly held 'feeder potential' for the three termini it then passed close to: Queen Street, Buchanan Street and St Enoch's.

The limitations of its cable propulsion, small tunnel size, peculiar 4-foot gauge and light rails, short platforms, high manning levels, and antagonised workforce together with the inability to adjust operational capacity to the fluctuations in daily demand meant any investment represented significant barriers at the best of times and with the wide spread drop in patronage experienced in the early 1920s ensured no post-war private bid was forthcoming. Concerning the choice of cable, Hamilton Ellis commented:

> ... to its ultimate great cost the Glasgow District Subway equipped with cable traction. [*Encyclopaedia of World Railways*]

At the Annual General Meeting in March 1921, the directors secured the support of shareholders to close the Subway if it was in their future best interests to do so. It was in early 1922 that company directors, which incidentally had changed its name changed to Glasgow Subway Railway Company (GSRC) to clarify its position as a railway, entered into negotiations with Glasgow Corporation with the view to their possible takeover. The Corporation, represented by James Dalrymple, the General Manager of the Tramways Department, knew they were in a strong negotiating position, despite this in good faith (and to maintain service) they agreed to subsidise the Subway's weekly running costs while both sides endeavoured to conclude the sale. These negotiations broke down in March after the Corporation's final offer of £300,000 was rejected; the company reasoned it was only just enough to cover debts and obligations but left investors with nothing and thus fell short of their owners' requirements. The Subway closed on 25 March, although the directors continued their talks with the Corporation knowing that they could not possibly raise more than the property value of the Subway elsewhere. In June the directors agreed to accept £385,000, representing one shilling in the pound return for the original investors (5p in today's money).

5: Glasgow Corporation 1922–1977

The Corporation officially inaugurated the system on 3 July 1922, and after electrification it was subsequently renamed the Glasgow Underground. The majority of former Subway Company staff retained their jobs, with hours and wages aligned with the tramway and the assurance that both systems would complement one another rather than compete. Indeed, tram services deemed as competitive were immediately altered; this may have represented the first occasion the city's various transit undertakings co-operated, as before the competitive ethos was very evident.

Underground fares were aligned with the trams 1d for four stations and 1½d for more than four stops and a similar season ticket arrangement. The takeover was finally confirmed with the approval in 1923 of the Glasgow Corporation Subway Confirmation Act. James Dalrymple, now joint Subway and Tramways Manager, quickly commissioned a feasibility study to estimate the costs of electrification; it concluded that such work would exceed £1 million.

W. C. Easton Report, 5 July 1924

The first report into the future of the Subway was to the Tramways Committee by W. C. Easton C. E. in 1924. After reviewing how similar city transit systems developed over time, the continued traffic bottlenecks on the Clyde bridges and the need to serve ever dispersed housing developments, Easton concluded that Glasgow needed what he termed a:

> ... first class, fast and high-frequency 'tube' service electrically worked with the standard gauge of 4 feet 8½ inches, but with a car little smaller than that in use in London.

Adding that as with Undergrounds elsewhere needed to break, out and that GCT being the prevailing underground and surface transit provider was well placed to ensure the subway and trams continued to work co-operatively. Easton noted that to accommodate electrification, a significant proportion of the tunnel would require widening due to ground encroachment and the occurrence of 'rough' track bed workmanship, also that cable's maximum running speed was barely half that otherwise possible with electrical working. Electrification costs were put at £200,000.

Easton also identified key improvements required at several stations, together with a need for surface access sidings to facilitate car storage during off-peak periods and the possibility of converting the track gauge to 4 feet 7¾ inches (local tram gauge) or 4 feet 8½ inches (standard railway gauge). An enlarged car depot was also planned but the costs, even excluding the depot, exceeded £600,000. Easton recommended that suitable new cars could be built at GCT's Coplawhill Depot, where the city's trams were made. General Manager James Dalrymple countered that there was no pressing need to alter the track gauge. With the depression in full swing the authority had more pressing issues elsewhere in the city to address, thus no investment was made and Easton's recommendations ignored; even a need to renew the cable stocks did not trigger action.

Electrification and improvement

In fact Glasgow was to wait until ten years after the Corporation's takeover before any advance towards electric power was made. Again the alternatives, in this case steam or diesel locomotives, were examined and were necessarily eliminated due to their excessive weight, since either would have meant laying heavier rails and track bed also reinforcing the tunnel shielding and if this investment were forthcoming the outstanding question of track gauge would still have to be addressed.

In August 1932 GCT fitted a pair of new compact Metro-Vickers tram motors to Car 60 with the view to evaluating the suitability of conversion. The test was carried on the Outer Circle between Copland Road and Merkland Street stations including the steep under Clyde 1:20 gradient. The programme was successful and concluded with a demonstration to the full Council. Duly impressed, the Transport Department received the necessary funds to convert the remainder of the fleet and install the necessary third conductor rail. To save costs the conversion process was undertaken 'in-house' the investment gave rise to operational savings such as the £10,000 per year spent on cable maintenance, not to mention the benefits of dispensing with costly Scotland Street Power Station. In March 1935, after a six week closure, the first electric trains ran on the Inner Circle. With the Outer Circle continuing with cable until closed for electrification that November, by December 1935 both tunnels were driven entirely by electricity.

Electricity was generated by the Tramway Power Station at Pinkerston, fed to the line via the depot, where car lifting equipment was run by electricity since the takeover. Despite the switch to electric traction and the reduced circuit running time from thirty-nine to twenty-eight minutes, the anticipated passenger growth failed to materialise. In fact patronage continued to fall from 19,969,000 in 1930 to 14,413,000 in 1935, not the ideal message to send to the Council – who were then the sole arbitrators of future expansion. A proposal for linking Robroyston in the north-west with Kingspark in the south-east was rejected in 1937. Minor technical improvements like installing compressor units in the cars to facilitate working new sliding doors and brakes did proceed.

Safe operations and the good working practices built up under the company regime were to be maintained and modernised. With electric traction came the 'dead man's handle' for electric train drivers – a fail-safe designed to reduce the possibility of accidents caused during running, e.g. where the driver is incapacitated. In addition each station has its own signalling. Passing through a red light is eliminated by 'trip arms' located at the entrance to each tunnel below station signal box. Should a train attempt to run past this device while the station concerned is not displaying a green light, the trip arm becomes activated knocking-off all traction power, not the separate lighting and communication circuits. In so doing the brakes are also automatically applied.

The fail-safe was proven during a peculiar 1963 incident, when a driverless train proceeded out of Govan, and sped straight through the next green light at Copland Road only to be halted by the system at the first encountered red light at Cessnock. Had it not done so there would inevitably have been a collision when the train in front halted at a station. Subsequent investigation found the driver at fault for leaving his cab and manipulating a bypass on the dead man's handle. It is of great credit that for the majority of the Subway's service there have never been any fatalities involving passengers.

Second World War Subway

From a low of under fifteen million passengers carried in 1935, patronage began to climb again. For the early part of the last century at least, Subway patronage was a barometer of local shipyard activity. The British Government, concerned with German rearmament, had begun to award naval contracts among Clyde yards. When war came, Subway patronage soared to unprecedented volumes; indeed, like other transport infrastructure at the time the service witnessed the draft of some of its most skilled workers to support the war effort, thus pushing the system to its operational limits.

The Subway is not deep, although near Hillhead the line reaches a depth of 115 feet (emerging from the mound to Kelvinbridge) below the surface while in other places it is only 7 feet down, thus nothing approaching the depth of central London stations, which doubled as ideal air raid shelters. Despite this, wartime commuters viewed it as a sanctuary from the surface black-outs. But the system's vulnerability was proven during a night raid on 18 September 1940 when a stray bomb (possibly intended for nearby naval facilities) landed on Beith Street bowling green south of Merkland Street, the explosion pierced the steel lining in both tunnels. Repairs were only completed in late January 1941, during which time considerable traffic was lost. The Subway was fortunate no further war damage occurred; indeed had Glasgow been subject to the blitz suffered by Clydebank or London the system could have been damaged beyond economic repair.

Post-War expansion plans

After the war patronage continued its rise; again more expansion schemes were planned. In 1947 another 'add-on circle route' was proposed. This took the shape of a similar sized circle featuring thirteen stations located to the east of the present system with joint interchanges at Buchanan Street, St Enoch and Bridge Street. The idea of this project was similar to the last, as was the outcome, with the Corporation ignoring the advice of its own Transport Department. The question of financial resource seemed more acute than ever. Indeed, few municipal concerns could afford to replace or rebuild housing, modernise essential city services and reconstruct a railway. The Corporation had re-evaluated their transport priorities and now sought to connect new housing estates with the city and industry quickly and efficiently; they placed their faith in fleets of double-decker motor buses, consigning both the Underground and tram networks to at best secondary importance.

The Ingles Report

In 1948 the new General Manager, E. R. L. Fitzpayne, described the service as a profitable asset, confirming that its 11-foot diameter tunnels, sharp radii tunnel curves and steep gradients meant the system was unsuited to heavy standard gauge vehicles.

In 1949 the Ingles Report on Transport in Glasgow and the wider Clyde valley recommended the replacement of the city's trams by electric railways on a suburban railway pattern together with the setting up of a co-ordinated transport authority. The Corporation was struggling to cope with other priorities and lacked the resources for extensive transport investments. They took the view that the transport services should self-finance but because subway and tram were failing to produce such, then no investment could be forthcoming. The Corporation's Transport Department was therefore forced to make the best use of its available resources and in the early 1950s five double-decker buses could be bought for the price of two tram cars, so again finances dictated matters.

Above: GDC Car interior, Riverside Museum. *(Author)* *Left:* Car interior, 1933. *(Modern Transport)*

Above: Car interior, photographed in 1974. *(Hugh Hood)*

The Halcrow Report

In June 1954 the Halcrow report concluded that an enlarged Underground system would benefit the city, but by then the sub-surface construction cost £4m/mile, while new near surface came in closer to £1m/mile. Halcrow recommended that the most feasible option would be a joint venture between the Corporation and British Railways in the electrification and extension of the suburban railway lines. Yet again the Transport Department found itself unable to respond due to the continued funding impasse. By now post-war patronage boom had peaked from the all-time highs of 37 million 1949 after which it began steadily losing custom. This decline continued through the 1950s and 1960s. The Corporation withdrew the last trams in 1963, only approving funds for the occasional station facelift together with absorbing the the now annual subway trading deficit. Among the stations receiving investment were Copland Road and Govan Cross. The modernisations that did proceed yielded frontages with trademark municipal aesthetics, including distinctive 'signature tiles' in part, no doubt, to similar architect and contractors being deployed as upon other amenity developments. In 1969, concerned at their on-going losses (and due to retire), General Manager, Mr E. R. L. Fitzpayne of GCT commissioned another study to determine the cost of widening the Subway tunnels to accommodate 4 feet 8½ inches standard gauge [Glasgow Chamber of Commerce May 1969]. The study merely recommended that such a development be avoided.

Top: The Broomloan Car Depot. *(Hugh Hood) Middle:* Electric traction bogie, with two 60 hp electric motors mounted on each bogie. *(Modern Transport) Below:* Broomloan car Depot in 1974. *(Hugh Hood)*

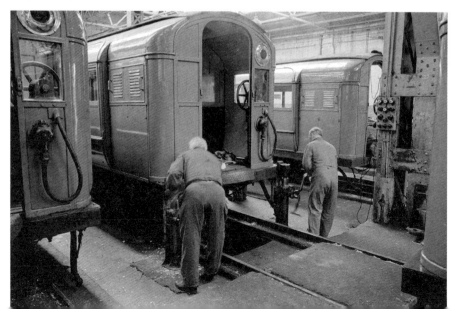

Hillhead Station front, 1950.
(Dewi Williams)

Right: Platform office, post-electrification, doubling as ticket staff rest room. *(Author)*

Left: Copland Road Station, showing passengers exiting end doors of train, platforms markings indicate anticipated next train entrances, 1975. *(David A Flett)*

Right: Car No. 1 at the Albert Drive Transport Museum (currently in storage), with recreated Merkland Street Station. *(Author)*

Below: Broomloan Car Depot inspection bays in 1974. *(Hugh Hood)*

Above: Copland Road Station with both trains waiting to go. Despite the natural light the station still appears dull. *(David A. Flett) Below:* Entrance detail of Car No. 1 at the Albert Drive Transpot Museum. *(Author)*

Above: Reassembling trailer car to bogie at the Car Depot. *(Hugh Hood)*

Corporation cars

After the Corporation takeover, apart from repainting the fleet in their then red and ivory colours and replacing the third wooden panes with glass, no rolling stock development occurred. That is until April 1933, when electrification required fitting the previous gripper cars with two electric motor bogies. This enforced partial fleet rest enabled the car interiors to acquire their first refurbishment, to include upholstered seats, additional electric lamps and white paint. Although the new electric bogies did have some sprung capacity car suspension was avoided, partly due to roofs being scraped at certain points in the tunnels.

The last new cars (grippers) were delivered in 1914; the system would not see new deliveries until the 1977 modernisation. Remarkably, most of the original GDS cars remained running. Perhaps the main contributory reason for this longevity, apart from good workmanship, was the fact the fleet were perpetually running beneath the city protected from harmful weathering effects; lack of any junctions meant that only straight running wear was encountered by the chassis. A guide to how many expensive rolling stock fleet renewals had been saved could be gauged from the fact that the City & South London had two renewal programmes completed prior to their takeover by London Transport, during which ownership a further three fleet renewals were implemented.

Make do and mend years

Lacking investment, the Subway was now forced to adopt a 'make do and mend' culture, best illustrated at the Broomloan Road Car depot, where most manufacturer car spares had dried up before the war. Engineers struggling to maintain thirty-eight serviceable cars were resorting to sourcing replacement axles and other chassis from BR or electrics from the scrapped tram stocks before intensive remanufacturing to subway specification. In another effort to extend the cars' working life, the original trailer units were taken to the Coplawhill Tramcar works in 1955 for body strengthening and straightening. It should be mentioned that BR generally renewed its rolling stock every eight to ten years, due in part to the anticipated rise in the cost of maintenance; no surprise therefore that maintaining this vintage fleet in running order was comparatively more expensive than any other similarly sized rail network, not to mention the additional staff requirements for employing a driver and guard for each train, augmented at each station with staff to manage the antiquated ticketing arrangements. One change put into effect was the adoption of the all-over red car scheme; it's not known whether this was a 'make-over' of the old stock or to emulate the by now public owned London Transport 'cousins', who were also suffering post-war lack of investment.

The manner in which well intentioned reports were dismissed or ignored indicates that at this time under the Corporation there was clearly a lack of vision and leadership concerning the expansion potential and the use of the service as an economic driver to aid urban development of depressed neighbourhoods in, for example, the eastern fringes of the city.

Transfer to the Transport Executive

Despite the intensive efforts at keeping their first generation rolling stock going, age related breakdowns were inevitable and occurring with increasing regularity. As were empty platforms, fewer queues and increasingly grimy station interiors and dilapidated frontages, all a familiar sight in the 1970s subway. In 1973 the Greater Glasgow Passenger Transport Executive (GGPTE) took over the Corporation's public transport functions, including the ownership and operational aspects of both subway and the bus network and necessary supporting infrastructure.

GGPTE immediately inherited a patronage drop below 16 million in 1973 although, like other public transport options, lost patronage could be blamed upon consumer lifestyle choices such as the rise in vehicle ownership, itself brought about by the rise in disposable income, enabling car owners to reduce their dependency on public transport. But the subway suffered from additional problems, specifically the decline in industries around the upper Clyde. West Street station was now virtually deserted between rush hours. Bridge Street and Cowcaddens were amongst several stations that were island-like features amid a desolate wasteland where the surrounding housing stock had been demolished.

Post-war developments such as locating new housing estates further from the city centre (e.g. Castlemilk, Springburn) and the satellite towns of Cumbernauld and East Kilbride, with either the closing down or relocation of industry to new industrial estates, had siphoned off significant subway traffic. Those that stayed were like the local community, in sharp decline; meanwhile those that relocated away from the underground's reach, if still reliant upon public transport, found themselves taking either suburban trains or more efficient point to point bus journeys.

Partly due to the need to demolish dilapidated buildings, a critical time gap opened between bulldozers moving out and builders or developers moving in. Indeed, whole streets and housing blocks demolished near stations in the late 1960s were still awaiting redevelopment in the 1970s. This had the effect of destroying local social fabric with housing, amenities, places of work and even entertainment severely impacted.

Buses had long since accounted for the greater volume of patronage and bus fleets were regularly maintained and replaced. In contrast the subway was anything but inviting: stations were now unsightly, facilities outdated, no inducements or plans were evident for passenger retention let alone to attract new users. Coincidently, around this time passengers were discouraged from taking photographs.

GGPTE control bestowed some benefits, such as reducing the threat of direct competition from the bus network. An interesting footnote regarding buses,was that even before they separated from GGPTE under bus deregulation, their patronage too was now gradually eroding. London Underground had been a Government concern since 1933 (initially also including the capital's bus and tram network); along with BR they derived infrastructure funding from central Government not local payers; in contrast; Glasgow Corporation was expected to fund all manner of functions necessary to maintain a modern city, deriving funds mostly from local rate payers.

Original cars awaiting scrapping at the Beamish Museum in 1979. *(David Jones)*

Investment finally arrives

A Greater Glasgow Transportation Study of 1969 simply recommended retention of the Subway in its existing form and nothing more. The following year a report by Sir William Halcrow & Partners (civil engineers) offered three courses of action:

- Give the system a minor cosmetic facelift
- Modernise with the view to offering a 50 per cent increase in capacity
- Closure

A year on from this, in 1971, another consultant was engaged for an additional professional view. That report summarised their findings:

> The present system is extremely un-commercial. It is life-expired; service failures are becoming more frequent despite intensive efforts by staff to keep trains running. To the public the stations are unattractive incidence of long stairs at most stations is forbidding and the journeys on the trains uncomfortable and relatively slow.
>
> The fare system is geared to bus staging and as a result is inflexible. The Depot is old fashioned and urgently requires modernisation. The principal feature which militates against operation is dependent upon a crane to remove or introduce train sets on to the circuit (the delay) means the same basic number of trains work all day.

The report went on to suggest that low staff morale reflected their working environment, which was a threat to safety. GGPTE responded with a proposal that the system be gutted and completely rebuilt from scratch. In January 1974 the Scottish Office supported their application for a 75 per cent infrastructure grant towards the then estimated £11 million underground modernisation costs. The service, which was clearly facing the reality of closure, was now being ear-marked for modernisation, commencing in 1977.

Partick Cross platform, photographed in 1977. *(Kyle Hulme)*

6: Modernisation programs

The 1935 electrification and tunnel sealing programmes marked the beginning of the service's intermittent refurbishment programmes. Due to the apparent lack of resources, Corporation development was to follow a piecemeal rather than extensive system refurbishment basis. Transfer to the Greater Glasgow Passenger Transport Executive (GGPTE) ensured the Subway stayed in public ownership and its successor bodies meant that Government support for infrastructure development, as with London Underground, would be forthcoming.

The PTE plan was not just confined to solving Glasgow's urban transport problems. In close co-operation with the then Strathclyde Regional Council (SRC), their aim was to provide an integrated and co-ordinated transport structure which would eliminate waste while gearing local transport to industrial and social needs across Strathclyde. Previous transport undertakings, such as the Scottish Bus Group and BR, tended to compete with one another rather than focus upon serving customer needs. So starting at the centre of the system, the PTE's aim was to iron out old transport bottlenecks and generally get the region moving more effectively – a priority being to eliminate barriers to previously awkward cross-city journeys to ensure multiple integrated modes of travel worked. Therefore the modernisation of the Subway was viewed as a core development for Glasgow's integration.

The first major modernisation, 1977–1980

The GGPTE announced the Subway modernisation programme on 25 January 1974. Under the original plan the intention had been to maintain one operational circle. However, public safety was uppermost and expert opinion advised full closure,. Therefore on 21 May 1977, and after 81 years of almost non-stop operations, the Victorian era rolling stock finally made their last circuits before a total system closure. In an effort to retain the remains of their patronage during the closure, GGPTE provided a temporary cover bus service; No. 66 was the 'Inner', while No. 99 was the outer circle service.

Renewal

The modernisation represented an opportunity to renew almost everything in order to resolve the former bottlenecks, inefficiencies and safety concerns that had plagued the system in recent years. Everything, except tunnel structures (and therefore the track guage) and electrical sub-stations, was to be renewed. In the main this consisted of:

1. Refurbishment or rebuilding of all fifteen stations, to include automatic ticketing, closed circuit CCTV monitoring and public address system.
2. Interchange at Partickhill BR at Merkland Street, necessitating the closure and relocation of Merkland station (which reopened as 'Partick').
3. Buchanan Street travelator link with Queen Street Railway Station.

4. St Enoch, and Govan Cross (now called Govan) to interchange with bus network.

5. Complete 4-foot track and track bed renewal, new power supply, new signalling system and internal communications.

6. New rolling stock in the form of thirty-three new one-man Automatic Train Operation electric powered cars capable of a circuiting in twenty-two minutes.

7. Broomloan Depot remained the focus of maintenance aspects renewed and extended, featuring ramped access to tunnels, stores, workshop, car stabling shed buildings and a battery powered engines for maintenance purposes and finally the addition of an operations control room.

8. Finally, staff uniforms returned to the dark brown reminiscent of the GDS era.

Above: Copland Road's second entrance showing a strong Art Deco influence. *(Kyle Hulme) Below:* 1978 perspective drawing of Ibrox Station. *(Alexander Duncan Bell, Architectural Illustrator, Edinburgh)*

Above: St Enoch Station main entrance in 1950. *(Dewi Williams) Below:* St Enoch South, plan 1977. *(Alexander Duncan Bell, Architectural Illustrator, Edinburgh)*

Reopening

Once initial snagging issues were resolved, the Subway reopened on 16 April 1980; this was some five months after the Queen's commemorative opening on 1 November 1979. That same day Her Majesty also reopened the nearby low level Argyle, or 'Trans-Clyde' line (originally planned by the Glasgow Central Railway), thereby again re-linking the city's north-west to south-east surface rail networks. Again the costs considerably underestimated, the initial 1976 £12 million Subway estimate spiralling to £42 million upon completion; despite significant greater complexity the schedules at both St Enoch's and Buchanan Street held.

Upon reopening both lines, the PTE emphasised that the combined Subway and low level BR lines ensured that 80–90 per cent of the jobs and retail shopping areas were then within a five minute walk of a station. This redevelopment of the inner city transport system was viewed as an important catalyst in the goal towards regenerating areas around formerly run-down stations while greatly improving the mobility of labour around the city. It goes a long way towards providing alternative transport for car owners and also advances transport planning policy that seeks to restrain the use of private vehicles in the city centre. The city's motorway infrastructure, including the ten lane Kingston bridge, has considerably eased the issue of surface vehicle congestion, and the city's higher than average unemployment levels are also thought to act as a suppressor upon vehicle ownership.

New stations

Passengers don't tend to notice the various mechanisms and procedures designed to ensure safety; their perspective is skewed more to their immediate needs: service frequency, clean stations, comfy trains and of course cost value.

Key to all this are the first impressions offered by the stations. Urban renewal, a ubiquitous term seemly encompassing more recent Scottish clearances, ensured the PTE's station inheritance contained a number of structures only fit for demolition. Exceptions included the relatively recently rebuilt and modernist St George's Cross (1971) while site considerations at Cessnock and Kelvinhall ensured they returned in a more recognisable form.

Architects Holford Associates based their work on detailed surveys of stations over Europe and Canada. The external results are both varied and individual. Despite visually and structurally variations, similar materials have been used again.

The new station buildings retained much individuality. Where there were external structures they tended to draw from a variety of different shapes, rather than being uniform block. However, to become recognisable as Subway stations it was important for the structures to utilise similar facing materials. The brown class 'A' engineering brick achieved much of that requirement. Floors and passageways are finished with similar vandal- and fire-proof ceramic tiles, brown or sand in colour. All handrails and ticketing barriers were in stainless steel. Not all stations could be enlarged due to extremely large construction costs. Where narrow concourses remained, Holford kept their surroundings bright and uncluttered, free from rubbish bins and platform seating. Overall the stations surveyed were described as having a pleasant subdued warm appeal.

Platforms, previously exclusively 'island' style, short and narrow, have been extended or flanked or replaced with side platforms for each circle. Escalators have been installed at most stations where there is anything over a reasonable depth to platform level.

Closed-circuit TV covers most public access areas. This not only deters crime and vandalism, it acts as a safety and security measure while also allowing observation of crowd patterns, so that train capacity can be added or removed as dictated by real time demand. New fire exits have been added to each platform,

Signage conformed to BR graphics and station entrances featured a large illuminated orange 'U' outside each station, raising the service profile and ensuring the passer by had little doubt as to the purpose of the building.

Signalling

The original company semaphore signals were replaced by state of the art BR units incorporating train detection featuring failsafe characteristics and fool proof alarm to indicate faults to the Govan control. The current signalling arrangements are likely to be changed somewhat with the arrival of new rolling stock, since these together with the control room function are being tendered as a single turnkey contract.

The second modernisation 2012–2020

For a time there was some uncertainty concerning the Subway's future due to the ageing infrastructure, including the almost thirty-five year-old fleet. Fortunately, the SPT – Strathclyde Passenger Transport was the successor body to the GGPTE – have secured significant funding to pursue a second modernisation programme with a £300m budget being rolled out gradually and expected to conclude by 2020.

The programme is extensive and wide ranging and it will encompass: new rolling stock, signalling and control centre, system wide station upgrades featuring the new grey, white and orange corporate scheme (as applied to the Metro Cammell rolling stock), new escalators and a travelator (moving walkway) at Buchanan Street. In addition to the new smart ticketing technology, enhanced architect designed glass canopies over the St Enoch and Buchanan Street stair and escalator entrances, tunnel lining and drainage, and power supply upgrades, together with enhancements to the Broomloan Car Depot, are also included in the package.

This investment has come amid a recent agreement with the unions for no enforced redundancies. The new investment will enable SPT to minimise its maintenance costs, with the goal of implementing fully automated driverless trains, to ensure a more frequent peak-time service. Taken together this investment contributes towards a more certain and secure the future of the Subwa

7: Infrastructure: Depot and Station development

Since opening most stations were either rebuilt or substantially refurbished, although West Street, Cessnock and St Enoch retained a semblance of their original 1890s surface appearance. Initially, most stations could only accommodate a two car train; the modernisation programme called for a three car capacity across all stations together with the introduction of flank platforms where site constraints and demand allowed. Similarly, where feasible 'embedded' tenement style shop entrances were substituted with new build, again site constraints created exceptions for Cessnock and Kelvinhall (formally Partick Cross).

Broomloan Depot

The original Broomloan car sheds which featured the tunnel pit access for crane assisted car lifting were largely demolished during modernisation to make way for Car Shed 2, a fleet stabling garage. Also located in the now enlarged marshalling yard was Car Shed 1, designed for overhauls and regular maintenance with overnight garaging capacity. Car Shed 2 normally acts as a garage for fleet but features inspection bays and overhead cranes, in addition to the works canteen and drivers' administration, with spare trains usually being despatched from here.

Goven Car Sheds in 1980. *(Author)*

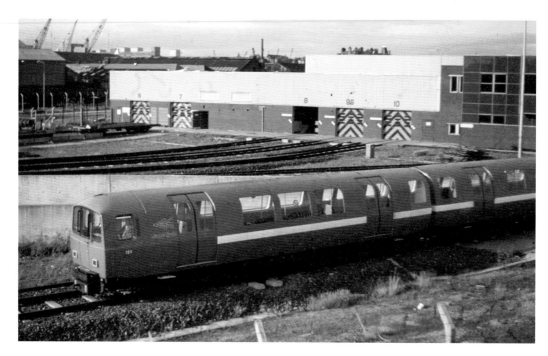

Surface view with a train passing the transformed Broomloan Car Depot. *(Author)*

The company stations

The company's station entrances looked markedly different from conventional railway stations of the era. The latter could be identified at some distance via several distinct characteristics: rail embankments, distinct station architecture, branded signage etc. However, this would not be the case with the majority of GDS stations, most were built into the frontage of existing tenement buildings, resulting in them often being indistinguishable from adjoining premises. In the inner city areas all the streets were already lined with tenement style dwellings. Most property owners exercised their right to sell to the company, resulting in a larger than anticipated property portfolio, thus contributing towards the need to utilise the various street level and basements where access passages could be built with the minimal amount of alteration.

As the route of the circle followed the street pattern for reasons of both economy (i.e. free wayright) and ease of construction, it was obvious that the entrance/exit should be placed at the nearest convenient street level opening. Thus eleven stations surfaced near tenement type streets and their access points were located at the most convenient point relative to the direction of the tunnels. As a result, some stations like the original Cowcaddens and St George's Cross were rather difficult to pick out from their surroundings.

Tactfully admitting that some of the stations were hard to find, GDS often printed station addresses on publicity material. Initially the tenement style frontages housed two or three small rooms at street level, which were partitioned from the public walkway to the platform. These rooms contained basic staff and station facilities, which were modified due to having to abandon turnstiles and accommodate a ticket office. Otherwise there was little else at surface level apart from the passageway that acted as both entrance and exit to the platforms below. Being of 1890 design, there were no fire exits.

Some not so deeply located platforms such as Copland Road and Bridge Street had glass roofs. Deeper stations like Buchanan Street had their arched roofs white-washed but due to naturally occurring dampness the intended finish didn't last.

Most of the passageways, all the stairs and the platforms were constructed in wood. After the horrific fire at Couronnes (Paris Metro 1903) in which eighty-five people died, the public were alerted to risks posed by such materials in confined spaces, earning the subway a dubious tag of being a potential 'fire trap'. Although traffic was on the increase at the time this well-publicised event possibly encouraged some patrons to switch to electric trams. To the Subway's credit not a single passenger fatality occurred as a result of their operations since the reopening, a record maintained by subsequent ownerships. The wooden structures were gradually removed by the Corporation after the successful electrification programme. Since wood construction was not common in London, one could only conclude its use here was simply an economy measure.

All fifteen stations had similar central single isle platform arrangements, roughly 150 feet long with the stairs located at one end and a station master's box at the far end. This was where the platform staff would signal ahead to the next station when a train departed. The box also housed a telephone enabling communication with other stations, depot or HQ. The platform itself was mounted at the top of a small slope in either direction. This gradient feature enabled approaching trains to slow and departing trains to coast until they gained a good cable grip. A third advantage was that bringing the line nearer to the surface reduced the stair climbing that might otherwise have been the case. Over each platform signage would indicate the shortest direction to each station. In the middle of this location was a prominent electric clock.

Ticketing

The original Subway ticketing procedure was for passengers to give their ticket to an attendant upon leaving the train, at the front or rear of each train, since the central doors were deemed entry only. The guard would open the entry doors while the driver collected tickets from his carriages' departing passengers, a station official collecting tickets in the rear. Only when all four gates were shut would the train be ready to depart upon receiving the appropriate signal. This procedure ensured trains would not normally be stationary for more than 1½ minutes.

This archaic and labour intensive practice was swept away in 1980 with the introduction of magnetic turnstiles, leaving platforms normally bereft of Subway staff with the exception of the drivers of the Metro-Cammell trains. The current modernisation has seen another step change with the introduction of smart enabled paddle gates supplied by Scheidt & Bachman, where passengers use ITSO smartcards to 'tap and go' through the paddle barrier. As before the barrier mechanisms are clad in stainless steel, a somewhat thinner design than previously, thus enabling an additional unit to be introduced where demand warrants.

Above: The ticket booth at Hillhead Station, 1950. *(Dewi Williams)*

New smart ticketing barriers at Partick Station. *(Author)*

Station infrastructure

Originally four stations were exceptions to tenement facades: Copland Road, Merkland Street, West Street and St Enoch Square; the latter was considered to be of some architectural merit. Merkland Street and Partick Cross were subsequently redeveloped, ensuring the station entrance was a tenement. Upon modernization Merkland Street was closed and the Subway access became part of the new Partick combined rail and Subway interchange as a new build in a new location. St Georges Cross, Govan Cross and Copland Road were rebuilt – others received cosmetic refurbishments. All platforms feature emergency exits to the surface.

Buchanan Street

One of the system's busiest stations, the original Buchanan Street entrance was a street level 'shop entrance'; it benefited from at least two 'facials' prior to the modernisation. The new Buchanan Street station concourse sits over the tunnels (mid-street) in what is now a fully pedestrianised shopping area. The concourse uniquely boasts three entrances: stairs to the south, escalators to the north and an easterly sub-surface travelator connection to nearby Queen Street Railway Station. The escalator entrance was originally open, however this caused weather related breakdowns on the escalators, necessitating retro fitting a glass canopy.

A major problem for the contractors was the near forgotten proliferation of sewers, gas, water and electric services accumulated over the past eighty years, which hampered the redevelopment schedule between the platform level. All such submerged services encountered had to be moved; once this was done the entire station and commercial complex was excavated to track level, at which point the opportunity was made to considerably widen the old station's previous ground 'footprint', with inclusion of a flank platform, while the former central platform features a barrier to ensure it serves only the inner circle. Precast beams support the concourse and roadway above.

Below: Buchanan Street Station in 1953. *(Dewi Williams)*

Buchanan Street Station
Top: GDS Co. Hurst & Neilson trailer 41T. A fuller 39T is exhibited at the Riverside Museum. *Middle:* Eastern entrance, with Buchanan Street inner circle plaform, 2013. *Bottom:* Travelator connection between Buchanan and Queens Street stations. *(Author)*

Buchanan Street Station
Above left: South entrance in 1980 and, *right*, the North entrance escalators with glass canopy.
Right: The South entrance photographed in 2013. *(Author)*

Below: Buchanan Street platform in 1950. *(Dewi Williams)*

Bridge Street Station
Top: The frontage amid the inner city clearance of the early 1970s. *(Hugh Hood)*
Middle left: Bridge Street Station entrance is partially obscured by its own electrical sub-station. *(Author)*
Middle right: Bridge Street design drawing, 1977. *(Alexander Duncan Bell, Arichitectural Illustrator, Edinburgh)*
Left: Former Bridge Street Caledonian Railway station. Originally the Subway would have emerged somewhere beneath blue shop front. *(Author)*

Bridge Street

The station location on the A77 is extremely useful for bus interchange; the area was originally a cinema destination and today it serves the O2 Academy and features a park and ride facility and serves the Laurieston area. Initially the company had planned to site the entrance directly under the nearby James Miller-designed Bridge Street railway terminus, then used jointly by various railways including the Caledonian and G&SWR. Possibly due to the anticipated move of those two railways to new termini north of the Clyde, the subway was located some 200 metres south on the opposite side of the road. The island platform featured a natural light roof that was filled in during redevelopment.

The station entrance is now set back from the main road, partly obscured by the necessary electrical sub-station, featuring a series of brick arches seemingly attempting to link both structures. The second building is significantly higher and serves to partially obscure the subway entrance from the main road.

Cessnock Station

Top: 1977 design drawing. *(Alexander Duncan Bell, Architectural Illustrator, Edinburgh)*

Left: Cessnock front arch in 2013. *(Author)*

Above: Subway centenary celebration image acknowledging the station's location beneath Alexander 'Greek' Thomson's buildings. *(Author)*

Cessnock

Cessnock station emerges under preserved buildings near Paisley Road West among a predominantly residential area, a feeder for the system rather than a destination. The island platform remains; they are close enough to the surface for the station not to require an escalator therefore the 1970s modernisation focused upon bringing the interior up to the then system wide standard. This included removal of much wall paint around the entrance. At one point a restaurant occupied the first floor above and vigorously competed for attention with passing trade.

In 1989, during preservation work of an adjoining Alexander Greek Thomson tenement, the architect suggested that metal arches be installed. The arches act as a focal point for a submerged subway entrance generally obscured due to its basement rather than street level entrance. The arches feature the Greek Thomson circle, mimicking the tenement stonework features. Under the recent modernisation the SPT actually removed one but was thwarted from removing the second due to a vigorous social media campaign aimed at their restoration. SPT described the arches as 'Pastiche not Greek Thomson or Rennie MacIntosh', but they did yield to the residents' demands and reinstated both aches.

Below: Cessnock entrance 2008. Stonework circles are evident in Alexander 'Greek' Thomson's design. *(Kim Rennie)*

Outer

S	
Cessnock	This Station
Ibrox	2 mins
Govan	4 mins
Partick	6 mins
Kelvinhall	8 mins
Hillhead	10 mins
Kelvinbridge	12 mins
St. George's Cross	14 mins

Cessnock

Cessnock Station
Left: Cessnock side arch and steps down to station.
Above: Outer Circle signage listing stations and journey times.
Below: Passageway featuring 1980s tiles. *(Author)*

Cowcaddens

The original tenement style entrance arrangement was demolished. The island platform was the only one on the pre-modernisation circuit capable of taking a three-car train. The station surfaces just to the north of the city's centre in a predominantly flat-housing area.

The new building reflects the GGPTE external treatment. The elevated road development has partially obscured the building from one side of the building. A tower feature such as that inherited by the adjoining St George's Cross might have been a useful idea.

Cowcaddens Station
Top: A desolate Cowcaddens Station in 1973 amid the excessive city clearing. *(Kyle Hulme)*
Middle left: Cowcaddens Station plan, 1977. *(Alexander Duncan Bell, Architectural Illustrator, Edinburgh)*
Right: Cowcaddens school of art. *(Author)*

Cowcaddens Station
Top left: Part escalator and part stepped descent.
Top right: Island platform.
Middle: Cowcaddens Outer Circle departure.
Left: Tunnel settlement distorting rail bed. *(Author)*

Hillhead

Currently the third busiest station on the line, this reflects the shift in travel patterns witnessed over some twelve decades of operation. The 1980 modernisation enabled it to offer a larger presence on the Byres Road entrance and, as with the other stations modernised completely, included acquiring an escalator and flank platform.

In April 2011 the station was the beneficiary of a £1.5 million revamp undertaken by Clancy Docwra, and it was purported that this was the flagship of the current station modernisation programme. The programme included installation of two new escalators; relocation of the ticket office and the creation of retail space for let; replacement of all materials on floors, walls and ceilings; new wayfinding, information and signage for passengers; DDA enhancements including hearing loops, tactile maps, tactile paving and colour contrast flooring; brighter, more welcoming energy-efficient lighting; finally a major bespoke public artwork installation by renowned artist Alasdair Gray, which consisted of a 40-foot long mural of Glasgow's West End told in colourful tile jig-saw style fitting tiles. Art at underground stations is not new but certainly Grey's use of jig-saw tiles is unique.

Hillhead Station
Main image: Station frontage, 1950.
(Dewi Williams)
Right: The refurbished entrance to the station.
(Author)

Hillhead's island platform with ticket staff, and, *right*, the steps, 1950. *(Dewi Williams)*
Below: 1978 perspective drawing. *(Alexander Duncan Bell, Architectural Illustrator, Edinburgh)*

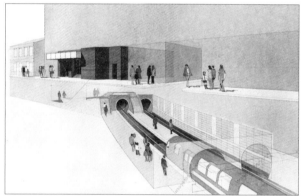

Hillhead Station

Above: Mural by Alasdair Gray, 2012.
Left: New escalators and stairs are part of the brighter station finish. *(Author)*

Govan (formally Govan Cross)

After the Broomloan Depot, Govan Cross station was previously the largest structure in the subway, originally consisting of just one entrance on Greenhaugh Street, which actually reached the platform via a passageway under the street. In 1953 a substantial new building was erected over that passageway, establishing an exit facility at street level. The original building was retained as an entrance and booking office.

The above arrangement was demolished because the modernisation programme required a major pit to be sunk into the ground (as at St Enoch's) to access tunnels and to create the largest above ground station structure on the circuit. This houses staff administration and centre. It is the only station to make use of fibreglass panels, used to brighten up the overall appearance of the building. Govan is an excellent example of bus and subway integration. All the local buses either terminate or pass close by; indeed Greenhaugh Street had been serving that function since the tram days. At the time of going to press the current SPT modernisation programme has not reached this station other than temporary signage.

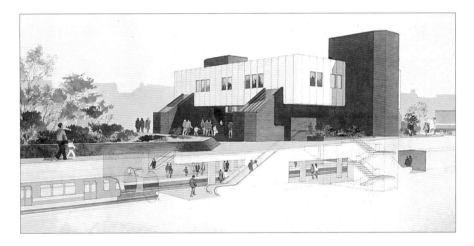

Govan Station: The bus interchange shown in the 1978 design drawing and, *below*, in 1980. *(Alexander Duncan Bell, Architectural Illustrator, Edinburgh / Author)*

Govan Cross Station
Above left: Exit to the bus interchange in 1970. *(Kyle Hulme) Above right:* The bus interchange in 2013. *(Author) Below:* Car waiting at Govan. *(Alasdair MacCaluim)*

St Enoch

The original St Enoch Subway Station, designed by architect James Miller in red sandstone from the Locharbriggs quarry in Dumfriesshire, is a grade one listed building. It has the distinction of being among Glasgow's oldest un-modified Subway station exteriors and is, arguably, its only aesthetically significant building. The exterior is positively crammed with Victorian excess in the form of Jacobean or Flemish Renaissance style, neo–gothic features such as corner pepper-pot turrets with elaborate finials and side half-dormer windows crowned with elaborate carved masonry trims. It is adorned with red roof tiles that, for many years, featured a painted advert promoting its service to arriving passengers of the adjoining railway station. The building's expensive preservation and reuse means the St Enoch Square retains a focal feature and link to its past when it was a key city gateway.

In addition to acting as a station entrance and ticketing office, the building formally housed the old GDS head office function and it featured an extensive canopy above the entrance area during the Corporation years; today it is no longer connected to the tunnels beneath and serves as a café. Had the 1925 Easton plan been implemented it could have been demolished to enable enhanced integration with the adjoining railway terminal. During modernisation consideration was again given to its removal, since it represented a barrier to station enlargement works below, but the aging preserved building's sandstone condition made this impossible.

The present Subway station concourse is now fully under the old listed station, featuring two exits, an escalator to Argyle Street and separately to the south of the square which had surfaced at a now removed bus interchange. Flank platforms have been introduced, featuring emergency exits.

St Enoch Station: Detail from Victorian poster and photographed during modernisation. *(Author)*

St Enoch Station
Top: South entrance to station and bus interchange, 1980. *(Author)*
Middle: St Enoch north escalator access. *(Author)*
Lower: Artist impression of St Enoch station *c.* 2020. *(Courtesy AEDAS)*

St George's Cross

St George's Cross is a retained name; the actual 'cross' roads as such was lost to redevelopment in the early 1970s, at the same time the original tenement that featured the entrance was completely demolished. Today's building is one of the few pre-modernisation stations to survive. The original pebble dashed concrete finish has been redressed in the GGPTE brown brick and for a time after the 1980 re-launch the familiar tower feature was adorned with the illuminated orange 'U'.

The concourse and island style platform were upgraded for the 1980 re-launch; the station has recently benefited from the new ticketing and signage investments.

St George's Cross
Top: Station plan, 1977. *(Alexander Duncan Bell, Architectural Illustrator, Edinburgh)*
Left: The station's brick tower. *(Kim Rennie)*
Above right: The submerged entrance to St George's Cross Station. *(Author)*

St George's Cross Station
Left: St George's island platform. *(Author)*

Left: St George's pre-modernisation. *(Hugh Hood)*
Below: St George's concourse. *(Author)*

Partick – previously nearby Merkland Street

The area was served by a station known as Merkland Street till 1977, when it was closed. The current Partick is an interchange station with BR's Argyle line. The railway station was similarly closed, having originally been known as Partickhill. Subsequently the GGPTE 1980 building has been demolished and replaced with the current cathedral like, glass clad structure.

Merkland Street Station was near the edge of the city's development, and passengers then emerged to view green fields flanking the Dumbarton Road. At that time speculators had bought up most of the surrounding area for housing developments. GDS held the expectation this station would be well patronised, especially since it was the last station before the line headed under the Clyde towards Govan. In anticipation of this and being the owners of the ground around the tunnel, GDS specified a relatively wide station frontage. The ticket office was located between a double doorway and a glass canopy was erected soon after completion in 1894 and this was retained by the Corporation.

Today Partick boasts flank platforms and was the first station to receive the new identity specifically featuring (in the all Subway part at least) the Subway's distinctive new white, grey and orange treatment. Partick is the busiest Subway station and a model of integration between the various transport modes – a westbound bus interchange is located adjacent to the entrance.

Partick Station
Left: Partick interchange, 1976 perspective drawing. *(Alexander Duncan Bell, Architectural Illustrator, Ebinburgh)*
Below: Partick as built in 1980. *(Author)*

Left: Partick rebuilt in 2007. *(Author)*

Partick Station

Right: Partick's new concourse. *(Author)*

Below: Partick Cross platform in 1977. *(Kyle Hulme)*

Ibrox – previously Copland Road

Built as one of John Gordon's plain brick stations and originally opened as Copland Road, it featured just an island platform and a solo entrance/exit. Passengers originally emerged to little development; it was to be 1899 before the traffic-generating Ibrox stadium opened nearby. The formation of the Scottish Football Association in 1898 was going to significantly grow spectator interest and lead to congestion on match days. Although being situated near the Southside housing schemes, it was only to be a matter of time before it too was in an area of high density dwelling.

Copland Road looked similar to Merkland Street but the demands made by vast numbers of football fans necessitated enlargement only implemented after the Corporation take over. The Corporation significantly upgraded it to include a second entrance way, with wider, segregated stairs designed to avoid crushing and conflict between arriving and departing patrons. Municipal architecture of the time reflected a distinct Art Deco influence, both inside and out. The new access and lighting proved the potential the electric Subway had for mass transit in Glasgow.

The Corporation's building was demolished as part of the 1977 modernisation programme; also the original glass covered platform was re-roofed to omit natural light. At the time of going to press Ibrox has just been made-over again in the new grey-white and orange station colours – results are visually spectacular.

Below left: Ibrox 1978 persepective. *(Alexander Duncan Bell, Architectural Illustrator, Edinburgh)*
Below right: Ibrox second modernisation entrance. *Bottom:* Outer Circle departure. *(Author)*

Kelvinbridge

It is characterised by being the deepest station on the circuit, and upon opening a lift operated from Great Western Road. The station originally overlooked the Glasgow Central Railway's station and yard, which prevented the company from progressing ahead to Botanic Gardens. Upon moderisation the old entrance was retained as the new fire exit while a new build was built on the former car park. Escalators were installed at most stations; the addition of an escalator to reach Great Western Road was a most welcome improvement at Kelvinbridge. Stations certainly announced themselves via the uniform illuminated pole mounted 'U' signs.

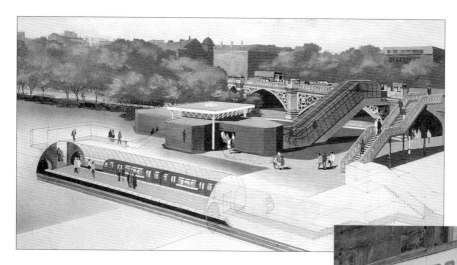

Cutaway and station plan, 1977. *(Alexander Duncan Bell, Architectural Illustrator, Edinburgh)*
Right: The pre-modernisation entrance at Kelvinbridge. *(Hugh Hood)*
Below: The Kelvinbridge entrance as seen from the bridge, 1972. *(Kyle Hulme)*

Kelvinbridge Station
Right from top:
Elevated station entrance.
(Kim Rennie)
Station exterior, and the
escalator to Great Western
Road. *(Author)*

Kelvinhall

Originally named Partick Cross till 1977, there has been no need for escalators since the platform is relatively close to the surface, down a double flight of stairs. The street frontage has always featured signage. The station was one of the first island platform types to receive the new modernisation make-over. It emerges to the back of a side alley off the busy Dumbarton Road, an area that has remained predominantly housing, with any vacated industrial land usually being redeveloped as flats. The station remains handy for Kelvingrove Art Gallery and Museum, the University of Glasgow and west end shopping.

Above: Kelvinhall Station plan, 1977. *(Alexander Duncan Bell, Architectural illustrator, Edinburgh) Below:* The concourse area prior to upgrade completion, 2013. *(Author)*

Kinning Park

Kinning Park station originally emerged in a 'greenfield' development area. The building was conceived by architect John Gordon, and the entrance was never a tenement – it was more garage like, remaining largely unaltered until demolition in 1977. Housing and industry eventually arrived but much was cleared again in the 1970s, in part to make way for the four lane M8 which split the community in two. This insurmountable barrier now has a pedestrian bridge enabling access to the south. The island platform is retained.

Kinning Park Station
Right: Station exterior prior to modernisation.
(Kyle Hulme)
Below left: The island platform at Kinning Park, partially illuminated by daylight, 1977. *(Kyle Hulme)*

Below: Kinning Park Station plan, 1977. *(Alexander Duncan Bell, Architectural Illustrator, Edinburgh)*

Kinning Park Station:
Left: The station entrance in 2008. *(Kim Rennie)*
Middle left: Seen from the bridge on the M8 motorway.
Middle right: Stairs. *(Author)*

Left: Kinning Park island platform. *(Author)*

Shields Road

The original station entrance emerged through a tenement in what was a healthy mixed industrial and housing area, located almost opposite the company's Scotland Street power station; it is actually located just on Scotland Street not Shields Road and a change of name remains a possibility. The city's redevelopment effectively killed off housing and any sense of community, thus blighting future traffic potential for some considerable time.

Much of the current patronage is generated by the adjacent 800 space park-and-ride facility and of course Charles Rennie Mackintosh's Scotland Street School Museum. The station backs on to a ten lane monster barrier in the form of the merging M74/M8, the nearest housing commencing about a kilometre to the south. Nearby motorway junctions do feed the car park with motorists reluctant to tackle the city's parking policies. The island platform has been retained.

Right: Sign for Scotland Street School, which is located opposite the station.
Below: Island platform at Shields Road Station. *(Author)*

Shields Road Station
Left: Station plan, 1977.
*(Alexander Duncan Bell,
Architectural Illustrator,
Edinburgh)*
Middle: Station concourse and
escalators. The modernisation
programme included installing
escalators on all deep stations.
Bottom: Station exterior, 2014.
(Author)

West Street

West Street Station was built in 1895 as a single storey terra-cotta brick building, with a tall chimney in keeping with the period and ornamental gable over the entranceway, and an island platform. Morton described West Street as a:

> Neat little building in red brick to the design of John Gordon I.A form attractive entrances to the Stations at West Street, Copland Road, Merkland Street and Partick Cross.

The station originally emerged in an area of intensive industry and docks, but was usually quiet in between rush hours. The station is almost dwarfed by the adjoining Glasgow–Paisley joint line embankment and remained remarkably well preserved until demolished in 1977.

West Street has two distinctions: by 1977, together with St Enoch, it was the only station not to have been embedded in street tenement arrangements. The latest patronage figures available suggest that it is the least used subway station. That however, this has not always been the case; before the decline of the area's industry and the closure of the docks it boasted significantly healthy traffic. Although there is negligible housing and a limited amount of industry nearby West Street, by virtue of its close proximity to surface rail, has featured in various Subway expansion and interchange plans, including the dropped Crossrail proposal.

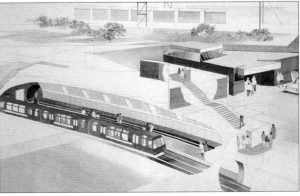

Right: Original West Street Station frontage, summer 1971. *(Kyle Hulme)*
Lower right: Station plan, 1977. *(Alexander Duncan Bell, Architectural Illustrator, Edinburgh)*

81

West Street Station
From the top: Entrance exterior. Island
platform in 2013 in pre-modernisation lime
yellow. Car 121 leaving on the Outer Circle.
Left: Station concourse. *(Author)*

8: First fleet renewal

The modernisation's largest single contract for was for thirty-three replacement state-of-the-art cars. The PTE initially engaged two Glasgow School of Art designers, David Brown and James Fletcher, who are credited with generating early images of what these new cars would look like. Around this time a dispute arose between the PTE and the Art School, resulting in the work being concluded by design consultancy Noel Haring Associates, who are credited with adding the distinctive compounded curve frontage with central doorway feature that blends seamlessly with the extended car body. A 35-foot mock-up of this design was placed on display at the Scottish Design Centre, St Vincent Street, in June 1975.

For reasons explored elsewhere, Glasgow subway cars have always been smaller than London Tube stock. It is not surprising therefore that feedback from the consultation exercise evolved around the standing room height. Some minor alterations were made, enabling the production cars to offer a 6-foot 2-inch passenger headroom, 4 inches less than before due to the 'kinetic envelope' margin that ensures the new cars do not scrape against tunnel walls. Standing height restrictions were a direct inheritance from the original tunnel diameter constraints. In most other respects these cars have proven to be a vast improvement, particularly, described as bright, comfortable and faster. Doors were incorporated on both sides to enable the new flank platforms to be accessed. Despite the incorporation of continuous welded rail, the distinctive subway noise or 'shoogle' (and smell) remains.

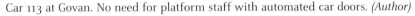

Car 113 at Govan. No need for platform staff with automated car doors. *(Author)*

Above: Metro Cammel car assembly line at Washwoodheath, December 1976. *(Courtesy ALSTOM) Below:* Metro Cammel cars in service, 1980. *(Author)*

Above: Tiled tunnel entrances. *(Author)*

Metro-Cammell

The new car contract was secured by Metro-Cammell (Birmingham) in 1975, a successor to the Oldbury Carriage & Wagon Co. suppliers of the original gripper cars in 1896–97. The new cars were fully automatic, not requiring a conductor, guard or driver. But in part due to Union pressure and seemingly part public reassurance, drivers have been retained even though they are generally hands free on the circuit except when supervising door control and applying the horn for unwary passengers who stray too close to the platform edge. Trackside mounted beacons are located around the system which transmit speed commands upon passing ensuring trains enter stations, or sharp curves at a pre-determined speed profile for that length of track.

The trains offer the flexibility of single, double or three car running with a rush hour wait of only four minutes. The ramped entry to the car depot enables near instant adjustments to or from the circle, augmenting or reducing capacity as dictated by demand

All train cabs have radio communication with the Govan operations centre and a back-up system is available for stationary trains that upon activation trips out traction power to that section of tunnel, thus significantly eliminating any collision risk. All carriages have loudspeakers enabling the driver or control to broadcast messages.

In the early 1990s, in part to extend the service life, the entire fleet was shipped piecemeal to ABB Transportation's Derby facility to undergo corrosion removal and chassis strengthening work and at the same time enhanced cab skins were substituted. The opportunity was taken to upgrade the interiors and ensuring construction material content was compliant with now tighter regulation.

Above: Island platforms with much brighter lighting. *(Author) Below:* Radio Clyde advertising on the Hunslet trailer car 203. SPT occasionally features sponsored liveries. *(Kim Rennie)*

Broomloan
A series of Ben
Cooper's photographs
of the Broomloan
Depot Engineering
Shed from 2013.
Middle: The
inspection pit.
Bottom: Car shed with
Car No. 128.

More photographs of
the Broomloan Depot
Engineering Shed.
*(Top and middle by Alasdair
MacCaluim, bottom image by
Ben Cooper)*

The 'Clockwork Orange'

The cars were originally delivered in 1979 in a light orange with a white line, in part fulfilling the PTE's request to avoid controversial football colours. Largely due to the adoption of orange the term 'Clockwork Orange' began to get used in media and visitor guides. The shade was later darkened to 'Strathclyde Red', with the adoption of the 'Trans Clyde' livery, necessitating removal of the white line. In 2006 the SPT's carmine, cream with orange frontage and styled line was adopted; the last all orange car was repainted in August 2007. In addition a variety of one-off dedicated sponsorship or all over advertising themes have appeared on occasions, including the 2009 Homecoming, Commonwealth Games 2014 bid, a local radio station sponsored and other consumer product advertising.

The current orange, grey and white was the implementation of design work by Stand Design (Glasgow), and began appearing in mid-2011. The scheme ties in with the prevalent colours adopted for station refurbishment and modernisations that commenced in 2011. Retention of the orange is in recognition of the past thirty years' association with the colour.

Hunslet-Barclay trailer cars

Rolling stock history repeats itself with the requirement almost 100 years on for additional capacity in the form of a tender in 1991 for eight new trailer cars. The tender was won by Hunslet-Barclay. Their eight trailers were added in 1992 and they have no cab or traction motors and must form a train with a powered car. Today the SPT invariably runs a standard three-car service; such a train has a capacity of 112 seats, and space for additional 165 standing. Each car is 12 metres long and, under ATO control, trains have a maximum speed of 54 km/h, but are automatically limited to lower speeds for the tighter curves and other route limitations. The trailer fleet frees up Metro Cammell powered units for overhaul and maintenance.

Second fleet renewal plans

Recognising the current fleet is now approaching the end of its useful life, SPT are currently undertaking a tendering appraisal with the view to re-equip. Two consortia / manufacturers have passed the screening phase and expressed interest in submitting proposals for this critical turn-key contract.

If recent developments in London are anything to go by, the next generation of cars will feature among other things: impressive aesthetic frontages, regenerative brakes, and walk-thru cars. There is every chance these may finally deliver the driverless trains that have been talked about since the 1970s. With technology attending driver duties, it should not be much of a stretch of imagination to increase passenger capacity by converting former cab and inter-car coupling space into additional seating or standing room space.

Left: Interior of a Metro-Cammel car showing the driver's control console.

Bottom: The tunnel rolling stock often utilises chassis and bogie material from old stock. This battery-powered loco (L4) had seen service with Taylor Woodrow. *(Ben Cooper)*

9. Achievement and legacy

The achievement

Railways, tramways and in fact most private infrastructure projects of the late nineteenth century were characterised as being speculative and risky ventures. Underground railways were very much in their infancy in the Victorian era, yet the service offered by this fledgling company was second to none. Their poster put their achievement succinctly, as: *'the only underground cable railway in the world. No smoke. No steam perfect ventilation.'* Indeed, the Glasgow Subway never exposed passengers to intoxicating fumes. The subway was Glasgow's first truly rapid mass transit system, linking up the main line railway stations, joining both sides of the river, serving suburbs the surface railways had ignored, and providing a rapid link between the affluent western suburbs to the city. In doing so, its design and operations drew upon similarities with tram, cable and light railway practice. A cable era review of the system by Benjamin Taylor described it as, 'the world's first underground cable tramway'. He considered that the subway's novelty lay 'in the combination of several features never before found together'. [*Cassier's Magazine*, Oct 1898].

Kelvinhall Station island platform mid-way through the upgrade. *(Author)*

Above: Car 110 leaving Govan Station. *(Author)*

With the majority of journeys accomplished in under sixteen minutes, none of this mattered to passengers who were prepared to stand if need be, as many as 150 per train during peak times, in order get to their destination as quickly as possible.

The Glasgow Subway was only possible because of the immense vision and determination of its backers. They alone galvanised support, raised funds, identified and appointed top experts in their field, lobbied Parliament, overcome the planning, building, technical aspects, launch and operational obstacles. The almost non-existent supply base did not deter them from designing and commissioning their own rolling stock, an untried traction system (on this scale), even a power station. Indeed, had this endeavour been undertaken by an established surface railway conglomerate, it is likely to have been heralded as a major triumph. What really places their achievement in its true perspective, was that just months prior to submitting their initial plans to Parliamentary scrutiny the founders and drivers of this mission were for all intents and purposes just another 'interest group' prepared to take a risk. That is what makes their collective achievement somewhat more astounding.

The legacy

The cost of building a similar specification subway in 1924 would have been significantly more expensive than the sum paid by the Corporation for the company's assets. Due to significantly higher land values, and after thirty-five years, all of the private ground the subway passed under would by then have been fully developed together with soaring construction and underground tunnelling costs to the extent that such a project would not have proceeded under public ownership. The same Corporation had invested in the successful electrification of the trams; they clearly took the view that municipal interests were served by an efficient public transport system but paradoxically that ethos did not translate itself into real subway development during the critical window of opportunity when expansion would have been cost efficient.

The company was driven by men of vision with a steely, old fashioned, can do attitude prepared to financially back their conviction. The company's great loss was very much the Corporation's gain. The system had the potential to be Glasgow's bargain of the century; the surface property portfolio alone justified the knock down purchase price and the subway itself was to prove its true worth by serving so superbly well during the most stressed periods of the twentieth century. While other cities were actually expanding and investing in public transport, by contrast the subway's initial public custodians, who (wittingly or otherwise, had contributed to the demise of the original ownership with their tram operations) proved they were neither capable of matching their predecessors vision nor emulating the progress of their public spirited colleagues south of the border.

The repeated missed expansion opportunities under early public ownership leave a lasting impact. Prior to the formation of the London Underground Board its constituent railways had frequently planned their expansion before their initial opening, they did so at a time when both costs and permissions were not the barriers they have become today.

Since the 1980 reopening the almost continuous refinements have generally been well received by subway patrons. The main controversy surrounding the subway concerns its inherit inability to break out of its tight circle, either to run on adjoining surface routes or to link up areas of the city that would benefit from a similar rapid transit service, possibly making part use of abandoned or underused routes.

> Circular underground railways are generally not a good idea unless they link mainline train stations and airports; they rarely attract enough traffic to cover the capital and operational costs.
> [David Bennett: *Metro The Story of the Underground Railway*, 2004]

What next?

Like numerous transport bodies, the SPT is not short of critics. Peter White (Professor of Public Transport Systems at the University of Westminster) called for a rational reassessment of reinvestment in such a 'low-usage' system as a 'sensible thing to do' upon the announcement of the £300 million modernization programme [*Sunday Herald,* March 2013]. Closure would likely be the only option if public funds were not available to continually support such infrastructure. Such a closure would serve a severe blow to the city's ethos designed to reduce dependency on car journeys, and the likely increased burden on buses would be detrimental to their average journey times.

What the SPT cannot have much influence on is the continued blighted surroundings of a number of the stations. Until modern housing development rebuilds those communities, the subway cannot perform to its full potential.

The SPT doesn't aspire to directly operate large fleets or buses or trains, but they have done a fair job at ensuring public transport infrastructure is developed. Under their custodianship the subway is directly benefiting with investment that a private operator would not otherwise have access to. The current investment does at the very least ensure there is a future for the subway. On that final point lies the opportune moment for the conclusion of this book.

Car 107 at St Enoch Subway Station. *(Author)*

Island Platform watercolour 2011, by Alistair Watson.

Acknowledgments

This work would still not be published as it was not for assistance, which I gratefully acknowledge. Specifically I wish to thank the following individuals and organisations for providing help with research or images. Unless otherwise indicated all photography marked 'author' is my own work. Research assistance: the wonderful staff of Glasgow's Mitchell Library and Glasgowlife, Glasgow Riverside Museum and Resource Centre.

I am very grateful to Alexander Duncan Bell (Architectural Illustrator, Edinburgh) for supplying images of the stations from the 1970s modernisation (and also for my first subway writings back in 1980!). Alexander's images offer us a unique and technically accurate insight of the above and below ground layouts, and which direction the tunnels go beneath your feet! Photographs were kindly supplied by: Alasdair MacCalum, Ben Cooper, David A. Flett, David Jones, Hugh Hood, Kim Renne, Kyle Hulme, AEDAS, ALSTOM. Thanks also go to Alistair Watson for the use of his watercolour.

Lastly but by no means the least the family of the late Dewi Williams who, by their remarkable generosity at a very stressful time, made it possible to share some of Dewi's lifelong passion in the interesting transit places he passed through.

Useful links

www.spt.co.uk/subway
www.glasgowlife.org.uk

Author's notes

Generally I have used Company, Corporation and PTE or SPT to identify management. In fact the Subway has officially been owned or titled as follows:

1890   Formed as Glasgow District Subway Company (GDS), widely referred to as the 'Subway'.

1914   Change of name to the Glasgow Subway Railway Company (GSR).

1923   Bought out by Glasgow Corporation Transport Trams Dept amalgamated with tram service to form Glasgow Corporation Transport (GCT).

1973   Under local Government reorganization, became part of the Greater Glasgow Passenger Transport Authority, operating under Greater Glasgow Passenger Transport Executive (GGPTE).

1975   GGPTE absorbed into Strathclyde Regional Council, but retained GGPTE title until...

1980   when it was renamed Strathclyde Passenger Transport Executive (SPTE) Re-launched as 'Glasgow Underground'.

1996   Strathclyde Passenger Transport Authority (SPTA) adopted the name: Strathclyde Passenger Transport (SPT).

2003   Officially renamed as the 'Subway' again.

2006   Strathclyde Partnership for Transport takes on SPTA & SPTE roles, retaining the SPT abbreviation.

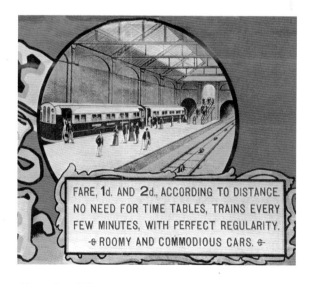

FARE, 1d. AND 2d., ACCORDING TO DISTANCE.
NO NEED FOR TIME TABLES, TRAINS EVERY
FEW MINUTES, WITH PERFECT REGULARITY.
ROOMY AND COMMODIOUS CARS.

Above: Detail from Victorian-era poster.